The Year's Work in Medievalism

Edited by Jesse G. Swan and Richard Utz

with the assistance of Alissa Stickler and Billi Jo Gronen

XVII
2002

Wipf & Stock Publishers
Eugene, Oregon

The Year's Work in Medievalism

Series Editor, Gwendolyn Morgan

The Year's Work in Medievalism, volume XVII, is based upon but not restricted to the 2002 proceedings of the annual International Conference on Medievalism, organized by the Director of Conferences of *Studies in Medievalism,* and, for 2002, Jesse G. Swan and Richard Utz. *The Year's Work in Medievalism* also publishes bibliographies, book reviews, and announcements of conferences and other events.

The 2002 volume is indexed in *The Modern Language Association International Bibliography.*

Copyright © *Studies in Medievalism* 2003
ISSN 0899-3106
ISBN 1-59244-381-8

First published in 2003 by Wipf and Stock Publishers
199 West 8th Ave, Suite 3
Eugene, OR 97401
http://www.wipfandstock.com/Publish.htm
for *Studies in Medievalism*

The Year's Work in Medievalism is an imprint of *Studies in Medievalism.* For the series, generally, write Gwendolyn Morgan, Editor, *The Year's Work in Medievalism,* Department of English, Montana State University, Bozeman, MT 59717. For volume XVII, in particular, write one of the following: the series editor; Jesse G. Swan and Richard Utz, Editors, *The Year's Work in Medievalism* vol. XVII, Department of English Language and Literature, University of Northern Iowa, Cedar Falls, IA 50614-0502; or Wipf and Stock Publishers.

The Year's Work in Medievalism
Volume XVII 2003

Preface

Jesse G. Swan and Richard Utz
University of Northern Iowa

On October 17-18, 2002, we had the pleasure of hosting the Seventeenth International Congress on Medievalism on the campus of the University of Northern Iowa. Participants from Canada, Denmark, Poland, and the United States of America gathered in Cedar Falls, Iowa, to discuss the reception of medieval culture in post-medieval periods. Four distinguished scholars (Verlyn Flieger, John Ganim, William Paden, and Bonnie Wheeler) presented captivating plenary addresses on 'Postmodern Medievalisms' (the general conference theme), and more than forty other presenters explored representations of the medieval from the Renaissance through contemporary times (see the full list of participants and presentations at the end of this volume).

For this issue of *The Year's Work in Medievalism*, we invited conference participants to submit revised and expanded versions of their conference presentations for consideration for publication, and our other calls for papers were met by an enthusiastic response. From the many submissions, we have selected those essays which, we feel, are not only fine examples of scholarship in themselves, but representative models of the diverse methodologies and topics currently of interest in the academic study of medievalism. Thus, each essay published in this volume makes a substantial and topical contribution to the field of 'Medievalism.'

It has been a pleasure working on this volume, not least owing to the many people who helped. We wish to thank Gwendolyn Morgan, the general editor of *The Year's Work in Medievalism*, for inviting us to edit this 2002 issue, to Kathleen Verduin and Tom Shippey for their advice on many issues, and to our expert readers for their help in the essay selection process. A heartfelt "gramercy" goes to all those who submitted essays for consideration as well as to those who agreed to be published once selected. Here at the University of Norhtern Iowa, we would like to thank James Lubker (Dean of the College of Humanities and Fine Arts), David Walker (Associate Dean of the Graduate College), and Jeffrey S. Copeland (Head, Department of English Language and Literature), for their encouragement and assistance. Our technical assistants, Alissa Stickler and Billi Jo Gronen, also have our sincere gratitude, as does Ruth McIntosh, for helping us proof the final versions of the essays. A special "thank you" goes to our departmental secretaries, Kris Knebel, Gail Moehlis, and Marcia Hansen, for their unstinting support. Finally, both the successful organization of the conference and the preparatory work on this volume were facilitated by Richard Utz's "Professional Development Leave" and his teaching of a graduate seminar entitled, "Studies in Medievalism."

The Saint in the Photograph:
Sister Marie Gabriel and Another New Middle Ages

Hannah Johnson

During the first half of 1993, a series of unusual newspaper ads appeared in several British papers. They advertised the earth's imminent destruction by a "giant fireball asteroid," detailed in a series of visionary messages.[1] Sister Marie Gabriel, the Catholic lay sister responsible for the ads, was preparing the public for the release of her book, *Supernatural Visions of the Madonna, 1981-1991*, and publicizing its most urgent message regarding the earth's scheduled destruction on July 25, 1994. As a result of the initial publicity, over 3,000 people made special inquiries at bookstores selling the self-published work,[2] and Marie followed up her pre-release press blitz with another series of ads shortly before the anticipated disaster.[3] The requisite pundits appeared on the scene, although the majority saved their most scathing remarks for the end of July, 1994, when Marie's cosmic deadline had come and gone without the promised end. Reporters filled column inches by comparing Marie to other apocalyptic doomsayers of recent memory, while a few letter-writers demanded apologies.[4] One man accused her of dragging humanity back toward "the abyss of fear and ignorance that was the Dark Ages,"[5] while another referred to the "long, dark shadows of Middle Age [sic] superstition"[6] that haunt her published ads. These references are hardly accidental. Marie's vision is shaped by a fantastical Middle Ages, a semi-hidden history that lurks just behind the text of her book, in the language she uses to describe her visions and especially in the imagery she deploys to illustrate them. In order to avert annihilation, Western Christendom must "return" to an authoritarian medieval past, retaining only the power of modern technology to shape world opinion. The history that saves, in other words, is the history of the Middle Ages, a blessed and draconian Middle Ages, a Middle Ages of tender mercies and harsh punishments, of ecstatic prayer and institutionalized restraint. In attempting to reinvent the past by refusing the excesses of modernity, Marie reinvents herself and creates a public persona of the saint as artist.

I. The Visionary's Moment

Christ and the Virgin Mary have been dictating messages to Marie for a number of years. As she puts it, she decided to become a saint and visionary somewhere between the ages of ten and fifteen, although her accounts vary in their details.[7] Between 1981 and 1991, she was instructed to warn the Western world of its imminent demise, unless governments took "draconian measures"[8] to stop the spiraling increase in sex crimes, pornography, animal abuse, and pre-marital relations. She outlines the substance of these messages in her book, and also offers details of various conspiracies against her, including the National Health Services' cruel treatment of her father and his eventual murder in a nursing home, the "accidental" death of a man who'd fallen in love with her and wanted to marry her, and the Polish government's refusal to return a number of properties belonging to her family before the war. She also gives detailed accounts of her attempts to give copies of her book to a number of religious figures, celebrities, and members of the royal family, usually without getting past the footman.

Marie is the child of two Polish war refugees, born in 1941 and educated in private British Catholic schools. She is now a tertiary Carmelite sister, and has lived in a London flat block on public assistance for a number of years, where her work is less than fully appreciated by her neighbors.[9] Marie's book is a religious account, a love story, an auto-hagiography, and an excellent piece of amateur P.R. It is also a work of intense nostalgia for a fully-Christianized Europe, for a British crown whose power is real and not just symbolic, and not least, for a world in which men and women are content to accept their religious and gender roles. Using found art such as prayer cards, postcards, photos, magazine clippings, and letters, Marie has created a scrapbook filled with montage, special reports and messages, and devotional imagery, all intended for the spiritual education of her readers.

While some aspects of this narrative are familiar – the plea for a return to more traditional religious values, for instance, or the diatribe against contemporary sins – Marie's work is not as easily placed (or dismissed) as the brief summary above may suggest. On the one hand, Marie's remarks about unsympathetic or dismissive figures in the church hierarchy recall a tradition of popular "exposés" generated by lay and ecclesiastical figures within the church. Malachi Martin's oeuvre includes tell-all books such as *The Jesuits* and *The Decline and Fall of the Roman Church*.[10] A former Jesuit himself, he now makes his living criticizing certain developments within the Church, stemming from a mixture of incompetence and deliberate internecine plotting. Michael S. Rose has made similar dark claims about the contemporary church in books such as *Goodbye, Good Men*. Other works, like the infamous *Awful Disclosures of the Hôtel Dieu Nunnery in Montreal*, or Marie Carré's *AA-1025: The Memoirs of an Anti-Apostle*, are more conspiracist in origin, arguing that the Catholic church has failed its own ideals, or has been forcibly subverted by the secret infiltration of hostile outside forces.[11] Finally, there are also those critics, like Father Nicholas Gruner and Michael Hesemann, who despair of the reforms initiated by Vatican II and make serious allegations regarding the church's alleged suppression of crucial elements of the divine revelations at

Fatima.[12] This modest list is hardly comprehensive, but in the absence of a sustained critical archive on such marginal popular texts, only an informal categorization of them is possible.[13]

Marie's conspiracism appears as one of the few links between her text and assorted other "outsider" writings of an apocalyptic bent. However, the discourse of this popular literary style is insufficient to capture the idiosyncratic nature of her meditations. Marie's tendency to speak in terms of revelation and the exposure of secrets largely does not extend to a critique of the Roman church itself, nor to the attribution of malicious intent to church officials and clergymen. She has opponents within the church and she recognizes them as such, but she does not posit a vast conspiracy dedicated to thwarting the truth, a common enough element in most contemporary conspiracist writing.[14] The lone exception is Marie's brief reference to the "big international cover up [that] has surrounded this story for ten years!"[15] This is probably an oblique reference to Marie's struggles with various publishers, including one who allegedly attempted to extort money from her by threatening to destroy her manuscript.

Certainly if Marie were convinced of a larger than life cover-up, it is unlikely she would keep it from us, considering her volubility on other topics. Marie's conspiracist anxieties, such as they are, operate on a much smaller level of personal paranoia. Random individuals betray or harm her, but she makes clear that this is usually from some obscure desire for personal gain rather than the result of a grudge against her. She is more of a weary everywoman with a sure conviction of the world's self-destructive capacity than an ambitious would-be academic seeking a grand unifying theory. In fact, Marie already possesses an ideal grand narrative, and it is religious in nature. She does not need to explain the world's inner workings in human terms — the system behind everyday events is already comprehensible to her in terms of God's will. In this sense, she is an ideal messenger, because she makes so few claims to knowledge of a "merely" personal sort. She is not in the conspiracist's business of research and fact-finding. She is in the business of delivering divine messages, or, if you prefer a more skeptical psychoanalytical vocabulary, she is preoccupied with filtering common intuitions, anxieties, and fears about the state of the world into a narrative about its end. If in doing so she echoes familiar millennial fears, we should not be surprised. After all, she is as much a product of her exposure to Western society as her strict isolation from it.[16]

The modern tradition of internal criticism of the church and the more secular discourse of conspiracy may provide a few useful points of reference with regard to Marie's text, but these are hardly comprehensive. Marie herself describes her work as part of a spectrum of mystical texts, including those of

Thérèse of Lisieux and Theresa of Avila, recognized saints within the Catholic tradition who were given to visionary experiences. Mystical writing constitutes an ancient Christian genre with deep roots, but Marie does not indulge the usual conventions of this tradition any more than she adopts the usual posture of the conspiracist. For instance, she delivers the sum of her messages from Christ and from the Virgin, often multiple times, but she offers very little information about the nature of her mystical experiences, or her spiritual insights. She does not journey inward for painful self-examination or questioning; she depicts herself instead as a prepared vessel, almost unconscious of any effort in the way of difficult spiritual discovery.[17] Whereas a great deal of older Christian visionary literature emphasizes the pious worshipper's identification with Christ's corporeal life, especially his suffering, Marie does not typically engage in such reflections. She also does not seem to identify herself using the familiar visionary tropes of Christ's wife, beloved, or daughter.[18] In fact, Marie's work seems more in keeping with the traditional role of a prophet, though she employs such rhetoric loosely and only in a few rare cases. The "girl-prophet of London" sees herself as a mystic first and a prophetic messenger second.[19]

Marie's inspired predictions are of a mundane, if tendentious, nature. If humanity fails to reform its sinful habits and seek a new way of life, God will destroy His creation. She often refers to Isaiah 24, with its terrible apocalyptic imagery: "The windows of heaven above are opened and earth's foundations shake; the earth is utterly shattered … the sins of its inhabitants weigh heavy on it, and it falls, to rise no more."[20] Marie does not address herself very often to questions of anyone's spiritual welfare; her unspoken assumption appears to be that if individuals perform the appropriate actions – passing obscenity laws, practicing modesty, and prayer – their spiritual state will immediately improve. Grace will touch them. Even the pop star Madonna, Marie's favorite whore of Babylon, seems to require little more than a week's retreat in a convent, reading and meditating, to turn her life around and become a believer.[21] Whether she is measured as a visionary or a prophet, Marie's role within her religious context is ambiguous. She identifies herself as a visionary, a mystic, but her writings about these experiences depart from many of the Catholic conventions for narrating these experiences. Instead, her text outlines a multivalent role for her life, as saint, recluse, counselor, and divine administrative assistant.

As we shall see, however, Marie's illustrations suggest some of the conventions of spiritual representation that her narrative forecloses. By drawing upon several medieval iconographic conventions, she authorizes her authority as a visionary while evoking the mysteries of the age she wishes to recreate. Marie's living spiritual world exists at a crucial juncture of the medieval and the modern, borrowing elements of both ages in order to suggest the awe and purity of the visionary's role. This negation relies upon the reader's recognition of essential visual elements and his or her willingness to enter into a dialogic interaction with Marie's book. For much of this iconographic analysis, I am indebted to David Morgan's work on contemporary visual piety, which stresses the role of popular images in the rituals and devotions of everyday life.[22] Of course, such a focus on iconography raises the question of still another cultural context for her work, that of outsider art. It is not at all unusual for outsider art to take religious or apocalyptic themes for its subjects, particularly since these are often marginalized by artists recognized as producers of "high" art. Eventually, it may prove useful to analyze Marie's place within this amorphous cultural canon, but for now, I have chosen to emphasize her relationship to medieval and neo-medieval iconographic models and her negotiation of these symbols in the context of the present-day world.[23]

II. Portrait of the Artist as a Young Saint

Supernatural Visions of the Madonna is strewn with pictures from Marie's life, from the time she is a toddler up until she is a young woman, perhaps as old as twenty-five. There are no pictures from her later adult life. Marie was in her fifties at the time of the book's publication, and told at least one reporter that she did not include recent images of herself so that she would not be recognized on the street.[24] Considering some of her prophetic statements, we have good cause for skepticism on this score. The iconography of *Supernatural Visions* suggests that young and lovely women make the best vessels for God's messages to the world. "I have seen a vision," she tells us, "in which God chooses a young woman, a convent sister, to be the new inspired captain and leader of the Christian church."[25] This figure is to be none other than Saint Thérèse of Lisieux, a French nun of the late nineteenth century, who is to return to earth for the benefit on mankind. Thérèse received her calling quite early in life. In fact, she elected to enter the convent at the age of fifteen, the same age Marie sometimes cites when she speaks of the beginning of her own visionary mission.[26]

Thérèse will begin a renewal of the church from within, because "the world is tired and fed up of seeing the church ruled by archaic old bishops, ageing senile old ecclesiastics who are completely out of touch with the man on the street."[27] Although Marie is explicit in her loyalty to the male hierarchical church establishment, she often suggests that women make superior public role models. In a rather surprising display of media savvy, Marie remarks that "the non-believing Godless masses would be far from indifferent to a church whose leader is an inspired, amazingly beautiful young woman apostle, filled by God with divine wisdom and dynamic spiritual powers."[28] Sister Marie understands the fundamentals of media saturation and the importance of charisma, including the need for an attractive spokesperson.

Marie herself has outgrown the girl-apostle's moment – the "girl-prophet of London" is not a girl anymore.[29] She can never be the dynamic female leader of the church, but she can be Thérèse's "spiritual sister."[30] Marie plays John the Baptist to the saint's glorious return to earth. She also contributes to the making of her own legend as Thérèse's earthly precursor by including elements of her auto-hagiography, fragments of a shrine that may one day be erected in her name. The Catholic church's ancient preoccupation with evidentiary procedures of all kinds is in evidence here, as Marie provides us with images of her family, friends, and favorite chapels along with a number of photos featuring crowds and "mysterious lights" around her favorite shrine of the Virgin in Willesdon Green, North London.[31] These images suggest the trajectory of a hagiography, highlighting Marie's special calling at a young age and her exceptional personal piety.[32]

Because she composes her own testimony, she is also able to show us her most "angelic" self, as a young, blonde, dynamic visionary sister. Marie says she "changed her dark brown hair to blonde because it looks more angelic. She is compelled to use some cosmetics."[33] In fact, the old photos Marie uses to introduce herself to the public (and the only photos released to newspapers), show a lovely, reserved young woman, gazing serenely into the camera, sometimes wearing her natural brown hair, and sometimes revealing her new bleached halo. She often touches up these images with ballpoint, giving her face the ideal lines of a silent film star (Figure 1). Like so many Catholic mystics before her, Marie sees no contradiction in her assertions that women are responsible for the evils of the world (such as pornography, predatory violence, the dropoff in religious education), and that women are the only ones who can save us from ourselves. She respects the church's position on female authority, having received confirmation of it from Christ himself: "Women cannot be priests, Jesus Christ told the London mystic that women cannot hold his body at the consecration … But Christ wants women missionaries."[34]

While she predicts that Thérèse of Lisieux is the coming savior of the modern church, Marie herself has not been idle in the fight to reinstate Christianity at the center of modern life. At one point in the late 1980's, she generated a sizeable following around a local Marian grotto in Willesdon Green. The London Times published a tongue-in-cheek report on a prophecy of Marie's that failed in 1987, remarking that the "spiritual reawakening of

Britain has been postponed ... after the faithful turned up in sufficient numbers to witness a promised miracle."[35] Sister Marie insisted that 500 parishioners were needed in order for God to deliver the divine manifestation he had promised her in a vision. She refers to this incident briefly in her book, lamenting that "the maximum number that bothered to turn up was 350 approx."[36] She also makes not of the hostility of the local parish priest to her prayer meetings, indicating that her efforts are not necessarily appreciated by the clergy.[37]

The shrine appears numerous times in the book, shot in different lights, featuring assorted groups or individual worshippers praying before it, with the frequent appearance of "mysterious lights" on the film. "Many hundreds of people came to listen to Sister Marie's messages ... near the London replica shrine of Lourdes [as she] tried to publicise God's final ultimatum to mankind and to all governments."[38] Along with these brief references to her own public presence, Marie reproduces numerous letters, scrapbook style, in her work. Most are from the personal secretaries of famous leaders and businessmen, acknowledging receipt of copies of her book. A parallel correspondence also appears, expressing interest on the part of various publishers and TV interviewers in the substance of her story.

Marie's perception of Thérèse's role – and for that matter, her own – already suggests the role religious iconography plays in shaping her visionary world. The images of Thérèse and Marie as young lovelies with demure smiles are intended to act as inspirational sights, attracting and holding the gaze of the public on the basis of their shimmering beauty and iconic poses. It is the iconic power of a woman's image alone that seems most capable of effecting change in the world. The evocation of icons in this instance is hardly coincidental. David Morgan dwells on the importance of "recognition" in portraits of holy figures, particularly Christ. "When a believer judges Sallman's *Head of Christ* 'beautiful' ... the picture's beauty consists in the satisfying experience of perceiving a particular understanding of Jesus adequately visualized. The image, in other words, fits a viewer's ideal."[39] By carefully posing herself at the center of photographs, and insisting that we read the mystics featured in her text as Marie herself, she is tutoring us in the religious rhetoric of the gaze, encouraging us to "recognize" in such portraits a generic sanctity encompassing Marie herself. Mazzoni comments indirectly on the importance of such "recognition" when she discusses the importance of an ecstatic's position vis-à-vis her viewers. Beauty, combined with the serene, frontal pose of the icon, serves to confirm the sanctity of the visionary herself for her audience.[40]

Marie's image of herself as a powerful female Catholic leader who nevertheless defers to priestly authority, is reminiscent of the difficult work of medieval women mystics, who courted ecclesiastical authority even when their visions appeared to subvert it. Unlike those medieval precursors, however, Marie has considerably more latitude in the permissive secular society she distrusts, and her representations of herself reaffirm the authority of her revelations directly. In one characteristic image, she pastes her own photo over the framed picture that formerly watched over the seated pope (Figure 1). He is caught here in a moment of contemplation, his hands clasped together before his face. She has effectively brought her own image into dialogue with the contemplative pontiff, taking the place of whichever holy figure may have watched over him before she transformed the photo. In the new hybrid image, he appears to be considering her message, while she confronts us with an earnest look from the far wall, challenging us to follow suit. Here is Marie's iconic self in action. The image reinforces her conviction of her special tie to the Pope. In one vision, she learns, "The main reason why providence chose a Polish Pope was because God has decided to choose a Polish religious mystic [Marie] to be Christ's messenger on earth."[41] Such substitutions are a common device in the pictorial depiction of saints' lives. Illustrations enforce a typology between the life of Christ and the lives of his holiest followers, but a typology among saints is also common.[42] Thus a depiction of martyrdom might invoke Christ's scourging, or the crucifixion itself, while scenes of ordination, preaching, or other activities might deliberately evoke the visual tradition associated with a much older saint. Here, Marie simply substitutes her own image in place for another exemplary model of sanctity. At several points in her text, Marie also inserts images of the Annunciation to the Virgin, and instructs us to read the Virgin as herself: "Sister Marie prays every day to the Holy Spirit of Wisdom to guide her in everything she writes regarding God's messages to mankind."[43] The standard iconography of the Annunciation is present – the archangel appears in the background, holding lilies, and the dove representing the Holy Spirit shines a heavenly light onto the Virgin's bowed head (Figure 2). Instead of the pure vessel of God's incarnation, however, we are to read the woman at the picture's center as another vessel entirely – the prophetic mouthpiece for God's urgent messages.

While this visual manipulation might appear self-serving, it reflects Marie's conviction about the urgent nature of her mission. The direction of transmission is unambiguous; Christ and the Virgin speak to her, and she is to speak to the public, government figures, and the pope himself. Our visionary often casts this assignment in familiar terms for the benefit of her Godless audience: "Almighty God has chosen Sister Marie to be his P.R. agent, public relations executive and his personal private secretary on earth."[44] More often, however, she speaks of herself as an ambassador or messenger, even a radio, dictating precisely what God has told her.[45] While Marie makes few assertions about the nature of her visions, their precise content, or her own feelings as she experiences them, we do learn that they often come "in the early dawn,"[46] and that she "decided she must try to become a great and holy saint" after reading the lives of the saints as a child.[47] Even her account of her first meeting with Christ is remarkably restrained: "He came towards her, and shook her hand like an old friend in greeting. Then he consecrated her as his apostolic messenger and ambassador."[48] Before leaving, Christ blesses her and issues stern instructions about the delivery of his messages to the world. There are no erotic metaphors here of penetration or spiritual unity, no overwhelming visions of Christ on the cross or the Virgin's tears.

Like so many medieval mystics, Marie sees her visions in terms of contemporary conventions. Whereas medieval women experienced their encounters with the divine "as it is painted" in manuscripts and on panels, linking their devotions to iconographic representations, Marie sees her own visions "as they are printed," in terms of popular religious iconography, often linked to medieval traditions.[49] Marie makes use of mass-produced prayer cards, wall art, and images from devotional books more often than any other kinds of materials in her book. The neo-medievalism and sentimentality of this popular art instigated a vociferous debate among Catholic clergymen regarding its quality and value in the first half of the twentieth century.[50] Such images have remained popular among Catholic laypeople, however, and their familiarity and simple spiritual messages are precisely what allow this artwork to speak so effectively for Marie. The glowing pastel colors of spiritual illumination and the expressions of rapt devotion on the faces of these painted saints speak to an ineffable religious experience. The pictures' use of medieval iconographic conventions such as glowing heart, frozen postures of ecstasy, and the play of light over holy objects encourage a viewer's identification with the images. At the same time, they suggest rather than fully disclose the mystery of profound religious experience, allowing ample room for individual interpretation. These mass-produced images allow Marie to intimate what her own discourse, hemmed in by modern limitations, cannot.

The narrative encounter between Marie and Christ quoted above is extraordinarily restrained in medieval terms – it seems more like the mystic equivalent of meeting one's archbishop than one's divine lover. However, this level of formality is in keeping with Marie's vision of herself as transmitter, holy employee, or empty receptacle for Christ's dictation, *and* it displays the influence of reticent modern attitudes regarding spiritual matters. If Marie is prone to visionary ecstasy, perhaps she feels it is in poor taste to show it. Perhaps she is wary of the modern tradition of equating mystical experience with mental illness and excessive emotionalism.[51] Marie's emphasis on the substance of her visions versus her mystical experience suggests an effort to frame her mission in terms more amenable to secular discourses of rationalism. She is far from speaking the language of science, but her careful attempts to dictate the terms of her public appearance, and her use of business terminology for her "job" suggest that her clipped spiritual narrative is part of an overall strategy of public presentation, one that seeks to avoid causing the visionary to be labeled (and dismissed) as unhinged. While Marie negotiates such distinctive modern conventions as media coverage and scientific rationalism, however, she simultaneously partakes of medieval traditions of representation, using her visual imagery to suggest what her narrative is unable to say aloud.

III. Reading and Seeing

Marie's silence regarding her mystical experience may reflect some degree of self-censorship based on the influence of modern prejudices, but this silence also gestures toward the ineffability of her experiences. While she is voluble regarding the predictions of Christ and the Virgin, she seems most comfortable relaying her mystical communications visually rather than verbally. "The Virgin Madonna commanded the London mystic to use all the pictures in this book to illustrate God's urgent messages to make it easier for ordinary people to understand."[52] The explanation itself is a venerable one, harking back to the Gregorian commonplace that images were the "poor man's Bible."[53] The pictures selected reveal a predilection for neo-medieval Catholic devotional art. However, in order for the reader to interpret these images correctly, he or she requires a dispersed cultural familiarity with the symbolic vocabulary of the Middle Ages. If these pictures are to work in the desired way, the audience must be able to take part in the ready identification of saints and sinners, the tricks of light and decorative touches that make enlightenment visible. These are stereotyped and derivative images, full of ancient clichés for the spiritually ineffable, but this is precisely what enables them to speak so clearly for Marie.

In one typical image, a nun communes with Christ at the foot of an altar. Marie's caption informs us that we are supposed to read the nun as Marie herself: "Jesus Christ appeared to the London mystic and commanded her to be his messenger and ambassador in Britain."[54] This caption suggests that Marie may have incorporated this image into her own practice of visual piety. She may have used it for meditational purposes, reading her own presence within the world of the picture as she contemplates Christ's messages to her and her own duties. The subtle accents over Christ's features, added by Marie in ballpoint, suggest lingering contemplation. A strategy of lengthy visual contact is a traditional one for Catholic mystics, and much Catholic devotional art has been produced with such an identification of viewer and image in mind.[55] Certainly we should understand that our visionary inhabits this image, she *is* the nun in the picture, experiencing Christ's singular attention. Despite her status as a tertiary "plain clothes" religious sister, Marie also includes pictures of herself dressed in a habit, making this "in-habitation" of the images in her book quite literal. The educational purposes of the image are also enacted here: as Marie literalizes her experiences through illustration, she educates us in specific modes of understanding. We are the secondary audience for this moment of revelation, but she is our proxy, linking us to the moments of transfiguration depicted throughout her work.

The symbolic range of this image is sparse. A trinity of candles tops the altar behind Christ's hovering figure, and rays of light stream from his hands and heart. The most powerful rays appear to warm the nun's face, while the skirt of her habit falls into shadow. Christ gestures toward his heart, signaling the intimacy and importance of his message; the nun clasps the crucifix at her breast as she receives it. We are told that Christ is issuing "commands" here, and Marie is kneeling to receive them, but the image surely suggests more than that – Christ's gestures are tender, the mystic leans toward him and her outstretched hand indicates eagerness and awe. The details are all wrong for a scene of late medieval illumination – the visible columns and the rounded arch have the look of a decorous nineteenth-century imitation of mixed medieval styles, while the tiles on the back wall and the floor would be more appropriate in a tidy bathroom than a chapel. But the gestures, the suggestions of medieval spirituality remain.

The nun and the magisterial image of Christ suggest an experience much older than Vatican II. It is because these images still have currency as the legacy of a traditional, "medieval" world that we can read them so successfully here, why Marie herself values them. When she speaks of a revitalized church making a successful conquest of the secular world, she is imagining – here, literally "imaging" – a return to the medieval, a reconquest of Europe's contemporary pagans and Godless ones. While Marie instructs us in the proper way to read such images, however, their evocative power extends beyond her own message. This suggestive visual vocabulary is also somewhat open-ended, allowing us to bring our own powerful aesthetic, cultural, even religious associations to the pictures.[56] Whether we see in them a distasteful sentimentality or the echoes of Sunday school memories depends on our backgrounds, but these are unlikely to be value-neutral images. They suggest an experience outside of time, a frozen moment of awe. It is nearly impossible not to recognize in them a lingering cultural message about the nature of contact with the divine.

Marie also reinforces her apocalyptic rhetoric of a battle between good and evil with iconographic strategies that evoke medieval conventions. The pop star Madonna appears frequently in this context as an all-purpose symbol of wickedness: she is both the incorrigible whore of Babylon and the simple sinner in urgent need of spiritual reclamation. The image Marie chose for her book's cover dramatizes the pop star's contradictory role. Several images are pasted together here to create an intriguing montage effect. The Virgin confronts us from her dreamy position on a cloud, an image probably borrowed from the back of a prayer card. She hovers before a quintessential British site, the House of Parliament, a neo-gothic space that already hints at the reclamation of a medieval tradition of rulership, blessed by God.[57] It is from London that the Virgin plans to broadcast her message to the world, through Sister Marie herself. In the space below the Madonna's feet, nestled among the angels, is an image of the pop star Madonna's head. This emblematic portrait appears throughout Marie's testament, drawn from one of the pop star's early incarnations as the "Material Girl." The singer's location just beneath the Virgin's feet signals her ultimate defeat, yet she is also a reminder of the possibility of redemption and the efficacy of heavenly prayer. "Angels and saints are praying in heaven for the conversion of the American Madonna," Marie tells us, and "The Queen of Heaven ordered that the face of the American pop singer should be placed close to her heart, in many of the pictures, for the Virgin Mary is a heavenly mother, who longs for Catholic girls especially to follow her example."[58] If at times the singer may appear to taunt and smirk at the holy figures who occupy the same visual space, this is an unfortunate coincidence, if also a suggestive one. Madonna's image and placement recall the medieval tradition of marginal art in all media, often filled with ambiguous or satirical characters.[59] This association is telling, since Madonna seems to operate in Marie's work as a double of herself, recalling abandoned earthly glories. In a few images from *Supernatural Visions*, in fact, Madonna seems to hover between the mystic and the divine presence, her head floating near altars or even sprouting from a rose bush. Pop star Madonna's role throughout the book is ambiguous, suggesting that Marie may be praying for her salvation but also that the singer is distracting or derailing the prayers of the visionary.

In another variation on an earlier Marian image, the pop star Madonna is tucked into the Virgin's sleeve, while tawdry adult film and magazine stars appear to climb the Virgin's robe from an invisible hell mouth. Here pop star Madonna seems to be leading the pack in an assault on the heavenly mother. In her original context (most likely a prayer card), the Virgin would have appeared to be lost in contemplative prayer. She clasps her hands together and directs her gaze heavenward. In the current context of Marie's montage, however, this posture of devotion seems out of place: now Mary appears to draw back, as if in shock or dismay, her posture out of keeping with the unambiguous message below: "all young women must change their lives: repent and become angelic saints to save mankind."[60] The incongruous effect is generated by the new context of the image, as Mary appears to search the heavens for succor in the face of the ascending horde from below. On the facing page of the book, a complementary image of the Archangel Michael defeating Satan offers an appropriate theological riposte to this ambiguous scene of the Virgin amidst sinners.[61]

Nevertheless, this overwhelming assault on the Virgin is appropriate in view of the book's trajectory. Sister Marie sees the modern world as an embattled sphere for Christian believers. Parliament is "a house of fools, idiots, mad-men and imbeciles, who caused the rising crime rate by robbing Britain of all its deterrents against serious crimes."[62] Law and order have vanished, while child sex abuse and murder are rampant, fuelled by "billions of tons of porn, obscene material and sadistic violent video nasties."[63] Despite their religious differences, Marie speaks highly of the repressive anti-crime measures adopted by certain Arab leaders and has made appeals to "the three kings from the East, King Fahd of Saudi Arabia, the Sultan of Brunei and King Hussein of Jordan" for their assistance in "publicis[ing] Almighty God's ultimatum" regarding drastic reductions in crime and vice."[64] Marie describes such measures favorably as "powerful deterrents,"[65] "genuine deterrents,"[66] and – her most revealing phrase "draconian deterrents."[67] In Marie's lexicon, "draconian deterrents" are associated with the excesses of a former age – a medieval age – of harsh punishments and religious discipline.

This reduction in crime is nothing less than an issue of cosmic importance. Like so many apocalyptic visionaries before her, Marie is privy to a global battle between the forces of good and evil, the outcome of which will either mean death and destruction or an indeterminate reprieve in exchange for our own effective self-reformation. Marie sums up the better part of her message succinctly:

> Repent. Change your lives. Give up drunkedness. [sic] Give up porn. Give up fighting, crime, drugs and theft. Stop wars. Stop divisions. Stop bad temper. Stop hate. Pray. Confess sins. Go to church, confession, communion. Pray daily. Do penance. Meditate. Read the lives of the saints. Follow the life of purity, innocence and holiness. Beg God for mercy while there is still time.[68]

Once again, Marie privileges appropriate behavior over emotional commitment or the experience of faith. Discipline, monarchy, order – these are the pillars of Marie's reformed, neo-medieval future world. "The sovereign will become … inspired by God to take over and purge Britain of all crime."[69]

In this cosmic battle, the pop star Madonna symbolizes much more than her individual sins. She is the very icon of an age of sinners, haunting portraits of the saints as a taunting demon and a reminder of the world's sinners who are close to their hearts. If Marie is conscious of the exemplary value Madonna's public confession of faith might have, she is also keenly aware of the harm wrought by Madonna's contemporary public image. The pop star's public persona is emblematic of a number of undesirable modern developments in Marie's book – lewd behavior, feminine indecency, and scandalous sexual mores, including the acceptability of pornography. Marie states that "only pure holy women can save mankind … woman's conduct is the factor which decides the moral salvation or downfall of man."[70] A few of Marie's images repeat the formula of the assault on the Virgin described above, in which an anonymous gang of women charges the Virgin Mary, but only Madonna is easily recognizable among them.[71]

In several other images, pop star Madonna's face alone appears imbedded in exemplary moral pictures, just above dire warnings about the spiritual wages of contemporary women's behavior. "The Virgin said a pop star who performs crude, indecent acts on stage is a puppet of Satan … with a mission from hell to corrupt the morals of young girls all over the world,"[72] while famous stars "are becoming whores, harlots, sluts and daughters of the devil."[73] This is the obverse of God's positive dictates regarding the virginal feminine behavior necessary to save all mankind. Our visionary presents an image of revolution, in which Thérèse of Lisieux's followers emerge as a powerful spiritual force in world affairs through their ideal behavior. It is perhaps hardly revelatory to point out that these portrayals are laden with complex contradictions. Marie's assertion that women incite sex crimes with their modes of dress and behavior is bound to strike most of her readers as obscene. But this is also a curiously woman-centered universe – women are responsible for sin, but they are also the key to redemption. Men appear largely as victims, victims of women, of the NHS, of unnamed assailants. Even great leaders, like the Pope or members of Parliament, have been led astray by the desires of their people. Democracy itself may call for draconian remedies. Marie states explicitly that woman's role is to inspire, not to lead, but her own rhetoric points to an active feminine principle again and again. It is this necessarily public, "missionary" role that has the potential to save the world from otherwise certain disaster.

Her own doctored public image – angelic, blonde, and lovely – recalls both the coy docility of Marilyn Monroe and the hard lines of the earthly Madonna's imitation of Marilyn during her "Material Girl" phase (Figure 8).

These photos of Marie's younger self are curiously consonant with those of the famous singer. Madonna appears throughout the text as the material girl, and Marie is her better self, the double who never appears on the same page as the singer. The images are a curious counterpoint, Madonna's smirking innuendo overlaid by Marie's demure impersonation of a classic blonde bombshell, both of them recalling a certain restrained-to-bursting 1950's "good girl" sexuality. By associating herself, however indirectly, with these more problematic images, Marie is re-creating herself as an icon, with an aura capable of generating sympathy, awe, and thoughtful contemplation. She poses herself for maximum effect, offering a picture of innocence and sentiment. The cultural models available to her (Marilyn/Madonna) suggest salacious inebriation, sensual overkill, and vice: Sister Marie subverts these images on their own terms, defeats them with their own bottle of peroxide, one might say. If the modern incarnation of the icon exists through celebrity, then Marie has grasped the fundamentals of the trade. She creates a salable image of herself capable of generating mass appeal, she tantalizes her public with promises of revelations concerning the third secret of Fatima and our planetary future, and she exploits available media, publishing her own book and generating press coverage. Whereas the pop star Madonna has used and consistently subverted Catholic religious imagery in her costuming and videos, Marie reinstates more traditional spiritual meanings in these forms without irony or cynicism. She reasserts the power of a neo-medieval, Catholic Europe by literally re-presenting it for us. She repackages "found" art – prayer cards, architectural drawings, post cards, magazine clippings – in order to show what cannot be expressed, that is the ineffable power of a life lived in the shadow of the cathedral.

PRINCETON UNIVERSITY

NOTES

[1] Sister Marie Gabriel, *Supernatural Visions of the Madonna (1981-1991)*, (London: Ave Maria Society, 1993), 272.

Textual Note: Marie's pagination is inconsistent – some pages were apparently removed from the book quite late in the publication process, so that the final version sometimes skips several page numbers at a time. I have accordingly instituted my own system, numbering all the pages myself from the Table of Contents, which I have counted as page

[2] Margaret Park, "Madonna v Madonna in a battle of spirit v flesh," *The Independent* (London), 24 January 1993, A1.

[3] Jonathon Sale, "P.S.," *The Guardian* (London), 23 July 1993, Features 22.

[4] Geraldine Bedell, "Become a Saint or Face the Global Cosmic Penalties," *The Independent* (London), 10 July 1994, Comment 17; Robert Chalmers, "Coming Soon … The End of the World," *The Observer*, 25 September 1994, Life 14; Simon Hattenstone, "Apocalypse Now, Or Maybe Later," *The Guardian* (London), 8 April 1995, Features 25. For the letters see Steve Connor, "Dear Sophia Richmond," *The Independent* (London), 14 July 1994, Feature, 21; Christopher Hilton, "Letter: False prophet of doom," *The Independent* (London), 30 July 1994, Comment, 9.

[5] Steve Connor, "Dear Sophia Richmond." *The Independent* (London), 14 July 1994, Feature 21.

[6] Letter: False prophet of doom." *The Independent* (London), 30 July 1994, Comment 9.

[7] Marie mentions the beginning of her visionary vocation at several points in her text. For instance, on page 24, she dates the beginning of her calling as "a religious visionary mystic" at age fourteen, while on pages 41, 64, 212, and 213, she claims her age was either ten or fifteen. It is unclear whether these references contradict one another or refer to discrete moments in her spiritual career, such as her decision to dedicate her life to God versus Christ's first appearance to her.

[8] Sister Marie Gabriel, 26.

[9] At one point, she appealed to an unnamed benefactor to provide bodyguards after being threatened by her neighbors (169).

[10] Malachi Martin, *The Jesuits: The Society of Jesus and the Betrayal of the Roman Catholic Church* (New York: Simon & Schuster, 1987); *The Decline and Fall of the Roman Church* (New York: Putnam, 1981).

[11] Maria Monk, *Awful Disclosures* (Salem, NH: Ayer Co, 1977 [1836]). Marie Carré, *AA-1025: The Memoirs of an Anti-Apostle*, 1972 (French ed.). Trans. Ira J. Bourassa (Rockford, IL: Tan Books, 1991).

[12] Francis Alban, *Fatima Priest* (Pound Ridge, NY: Good Counsel, 1997); Michael Hesemann, *The Fatima Secret* (New York: Dell, 2000).

[13] A fine example of the kind of work that might be done in this area is Linda Kintz's book, *Between Jesus and the Market: The Emotions That Matter in Right-Wing America* (Durham: Duke UP, 1997).

Certain high-profile groups, like the Branch Davidians or the Solar Temple cult, have received a great deal of attention recently from scholars and journalists alike. However, the sustained production of paranoid or otherwise marginal texts is still largely ignored by mainstream critics. *Conspiracy Culture* and the *Conspiracy Theories* are two books that attempt to address this gap in our critical lexicon using the methods of cultural studies. Peter Knight, *Conspiracy Culture: From Kennedy to the X-Files*, New York: Routledge, 2000. Mark Fenster, *Conspiracy Theories: Secrecy and Power in American Culture* (Minneapolis: U of Minnesota P, 1999).

Note, however, that these books deal largely with items of "political" commentary. Pseudo-historical writing and so-called New-Age texts remain under-examined. One notable exception is Wouter Hanegraaff's excellent study, *New Age Religion and Western Culture: Esotericism in the Mirror of Secular Thought.* (New York: SUNY P, 1998).

[14] Knight, Peter. *Conspiracy Culture: From Kennedy to the X-Files* (New York: Routledge, 2000), 1-9.

[15] Sister Marie Gabriel, 323.

[16] Lee Quinby, *Anti-Apocalypse: Exercises in Genealogical Criticism* (Minneapolis: U of Minnesota P, 1994), xi-xxvii.

Although Norman Cohn's oeuvre contains some rather problematic "grand narrative" elements of its own, he has spend much of his career analyzing some of the basic characteristics of millennial movements throughout Western history. A number of these tropes and assumptions are present in *Supernatural Visions*. See *Pursuit of the Millennium, Cosmos, Chaos, and the World to Come*, and even *Warrant for Genocide*.

[17] Mazzoni offers an intriguing comparative of study of a medieval mystic (Angela of Foligno) and a modern one (Gemma Galgani) which emphasizes the continuity of these themes in Catholic, feminine, mystical experience. Self-doubt is also notably absent from Marie's writing. Cristina Mazzoni, *Saint Hysteria: Neurosis, Mysticism, and Gender in European Culture* (Ithaca: Cornell UP, 1996).

[18] For a discussion of the early development of affective devotion to Christ's body, see Bynum's *Jesus as Mother*, especially her essay, "Women Mystics in the Thirteenth Century: The Case of the Nuns of Helfta," (Berkeley: U of California P, 1982), 170-262. See also: Mariateresa Fumagalli Beonio-Brochhieri, "The Feminine Mind in Medieval Mysticism," *Creative Women in Medieval and Early Modern Italy*. Eds. E. Ann Matter and John Coakly, (Philadelphia: U of Pennsylvania P, 1994), 19-33. Jeffrey F. Hamburger speaks at length on the tradition of "bridal mysticism" in Catholic devotional writing: Hamburger, "The Visual and the Visionary: The Image in Late Medieval Monastic Devotions," *Viator* 20 (1989): 161-182.

[19] Sister Marie Gabriel, 435.

[20] Isaiah 24: 18-24.

[21] Sister Marie Gabriel, 296.

[22] David Morgan, *Visual Piety: A History and Theory of Popular Religious Images* (Berkeley: U of California P, 1998).

[23] For further study, see: Roger Manley (ed.), *The End is Near! Visions of Apocalypse, Millennium, and Utopia* (Los Angeles: Dilettante, 1998); Colin Rhodes, *Outsider Art: Spontaneous Alternatives* (New York: Thames and Hudson, 2000); Angelus, et al, *In Another World: Outsider Art from Europe & America* (London: South Bank Centre, 1987).

[24] Mark Ellis, "Missing Faithful Postpone Miracle," *The Times* (London), 20 April 1987.

[25] Sister Marie Gabriel, 268.

[26] Sister Marie Gabriel, 41.

[27] Sister Marie Gabriel, 268.

[28] Sister Marie Gabriel, 268.

[29] Sister Marie Gabriel, 435.

[30] Sister Marie Gabriel, 269.

[31] Sister Marie Gabriel, 250-1.

[32] For a full catalogue of the typical scenes featured in pictorial hagiographic cycles, see Barbara Abou-El-Haj, *The Medieval Cult of Saints* (Cambridge: Cambridge UP, 1994). Woodward gives a modern account in Kenneth L. Woodward, *Making Saints: How the Catholic Church Determines Who Becomes a Saint, Who Doesn't, and Why* (New York: Simon & Schuster, 1996).

[33] Sister Marie Gabriel, 94.

[34] Sister Marie Gabriel, 78.

[35] Mark Ellis, "Missing Faithful Postpone Miracle," The Times (London), 20 April 1987.

[36] Sister Marie Gabriel, 252.

[37] Sister Marie Gabriel, 136, 205.

[38] Sister Marie Gabriel, 138.

[39] Morgan, 32.

[40] Mazzoni, 164-5.

[41] Sister Marie Gabriel, 209.

[42] Barbara Abou-El-Haj, The Medieval Cult of Saints (Cambridge: Cambridge UP, 1994), 34.

[43] Sister Marie Gabriel, 184.

[44] Sister Marie Gabriel, 95.

[45] Sister Marie Gabriel, 265.

[46] Sister Marie Gabriel, 95.

[47] Sister Marie Gabriel, 212.

[48] Sister Marie Gabriel, 168.

[49] For a few insightful discussions of this phenomenon, see Hamburger, "The Visual and the Visionary;" Sixten Ringbom, "Devotional Images and Imaginative Devotions," Gazette Des Beaux-Arts 73 (1969): 159-170; Chiara Frugoni, "Female Mystics, Visions, and Iconography," in Daniel Bornstein, ed., Women and Religion in Medieval and Renaissance Italy (Chicago: U of Chicago P, 1996), 130-164.

[50] For a brief history of this debate, see Colleen McDannell, Material Christianity: Religion and Popular Culture in America (New Haven: Yale UP, 1995), 135-62.

[51] Mazzoni, 17-53.

[52] Sister Marie Gabriel, 237.

[53] Hamburger, 161-4; Ringbom, 162-4.

[54] Sister Marie Gabriel, 54.

[55] Chiara Frugoni, "Female Mystics, Visions, and Iconography," Women and Religion in Medieval and Renaissance Italy. Ed. Daniel Bornstein (Chicago: U of Chicago P, 1996), 137-9; Ringbom, 160-2.

[56] Morgan, 26.

[57] Kenneth Clark, The Gothic Revival: An Essay on the History of Taste 2nd ed. (London: Constable, 1950), 145-63.

[58] Sister Marie Gabriel, 10.

[59] The most extensive recent treatment of this topic remains Michael Camille's Image on the Edge: The Margins of Medieval Art (Cambridge: Harvard UP, 1992).

[60] Sister Marie Gabriel, 170.

[61] Sister Marie Gabriel, 171.

[62] Sister Marie Gabriel, 148.

[63] Sister Marie Gabriel, 155.

[64] Sister Marie Gabriel, 232.

[65] Sister Marie Gabriel, 232.

[66] Sister Marie Gabriel, 233.

[67] Sister Marie Gabriel, 233.
[68] Sister Marie Gabriel, 265.
[69] Sister Marie Gabriel, 156.
[70] Sister Marie Gabriel, 198-9.
[71] Sister Marie Gabriel, 202-3, 307.
[72] Sister Marie Gabriel, 226.
[73] Sister Marie Gabriel, 257.

The Postmodern Subject in Early Christian Catacomb Painting

Mike McKeon

I.

Art historian Ernst Kitzinger has characterized the transition from Roman Imperial art (ca. first and second century CE)[1] to Late Antique art (ca. third to fifth century CE)[2] as a decline in artistic style and craftsmanship.[3] "Decline," Kitzinger notes, was especially marked by the craftsman's treatment and handling of the medium. For instance, Late Antique sculpture shows less skill as the artist manages to treat a figure as a single block of stone rather than articulating it.[4] And since less effort was needed to engrave features on a face, or folds on a drapery, than to model such elements, art from Late Antiquity, and for our purposes Early Christian art especially, has received the rather injudicious appellation of "decline," that is, in comparison with the classicized beauty of its Roman Imperial predecessor.

To characterize the art of Late Antiquity/Early Christian as "decline," I believe, contributes to the false perception of the Medieval period as a "dark age," especially in the technical proficiency of the visual artist. Moreover, to limit the analysis of this art historical transition to only formal considerations has been shown to reveal more about one's own critical stance rather than to establish an objectively valid claim regarding the nature of the artifacts representative of this transition.

While I am partial to multiple critical approaches with a view to art, I do believe that some critical stances do a better job at ascertaining the causes for why a particular artistic phenomenon manifests itself. I have, therefore, chosen to "refract," if you will, representative samplings of art of the Early Christian era through the lens of postmodernity. This methodological approach serves many functions. First, it offers answers to questions that contemporary research on Early Christian art has generated, such as: "how does the Christian catacomb painter begin to conceive of a new style of visual linguistics essentially at odds with the highly formalized beauty of classical art; are metaphysical issues such as human subjectivity, the soul and its relationship to the world and God, having some effect in shaping the artistic imagination of the Early Christian painter?" And second, this type of postmodern inquiry will ascertain answers to these questions through exposing the limits of tradition-bound formalism and iconographical studies as they have been historically applied to Early Christian catacomb painting.

To undermine traditional or orthodox explanations operating behind one of the most significant transitions in art history: Antiquity to the Medieval period, is not the focus of this paper. On the contrary, what I hope I might share are revealing clues about Christian art through identifying additional forces at work unforeseen by traditional art history. Ultimately, what will emerge from this inquiry is a "de-Medievalizing," so to speak, of an artistic movement that has been commonly misconstrued as a "decline" in technical skill and craftsmanship; and the optimal point from which to commence this critical investigation is by considering some of the remaining samples of artwork left to us from the Early Christian era.

Following an initial assessment of the form of Christian catacomb works, particularly from the tombs of *Saint Marcellino and Pietro* (ca. early fourth century CE), the issue of subject matter in Early Christian art will be taken up, and how it entails a representational style that re-envisions a new conception of human sexuality. Through a method of postmodern hermeneutics of the subject, the Christian self, I argue, is brought to light through the body's potential for sin and lust and the attendant shame and guilt that accompany them; moreover, by applying Michel Foucault's techniques of the self to the process of individual conversion into a community of Christian believers, a new self-identity emerges that shapes and delimits the aesthetic imagination of the catacomb painter in ways never thought before.

II.

In room 57 of the catacombs of Saints Marcellino and Pietro (ca. fourth century CE), is a representation of the Fall of Adam and Eve from the *Old Testament*. Both are represented standing with bowed heads and facially contorted features. They are spatially located alongside an impressionistic tree that bisects the foreground.[5] Despite the fresco image's strong but simple formal organization, the most salient feature of the painting is a feeling of moral crisis. Shame and guilt are suggested through the artist's application of a strong broken line across the brows of each downcast heads, and immediately beneath Adam's forehead a daub of triangularly shaped paint has been applied suggesting an emotional feeling rather than the naturalistic representation of an eye. Moreover, the solemnity of the moment is enhanced by the straight lines of the mouths on both figures and their crossed hands holding fig leaves to cover their genitals – the location at which they have experienced the first stirrings of lust.

In addition to this singular visual account of the Fall there also exists in the same catacombs three other representations depicting the same subject.[6] Curiously, as we begin to compare the three frescoes, what we discover in relation to room 57 is a complete lack of any expression of shame or guilt on the faces of Adam and Eve.[7] For instance, located in the arch-spaced entrance to room 52 is a representation of Adam and Eve standing astride the tree, both covering their genitals with fig leaves while the serpent coils itself around the tree. Adam looks askance from Eve; they express some growing concern regarding the possible gravity of their actions but without the finality and absolute awareness we see in room 57. Moreover, on wall two in room 44 we note the same spatial organization existing among the parts as we find in rooms 57, 51, and 52, but now with the added feature of Eve's arms extended toward Adam, as if to converse, a gesture which is simply reversed in room 51.[8] Both figures, in rooms 51 and 44, stand astride the tree facing each other while the serpent coils around it. What is lacking in both representations in comparison with room 57, once again, is any expression of shame, guilt, or recognition of disobedience on the part of Adam and Eve.

Jas Elsner explains how the similarities among these various compositional schemes were the product of an iconographical canon.[9] This pictorial canon grew to prominence commensurate with the distillation of a general Catholic orthodoxy around the fourth century CE.[10] What exactly was visually entailed in this new canon, however, beyond their formal similarities is open to speculation. Andre Grabar suspects that the generally orthodox views of the church on doctrinal issues, particularly the redemption of Christ, were thematically represented not in any one particular image per se, but within iconographical groupings.[11] For instance, the beginning of the fourth century CE saw the union of representations of Adam and Eve with other Old and New Testament images as demonstrating a "scheme of salvation" based on the new religious understanding of the doctrines of Original Sin and Redemption.[12] And indeed, each one of the representations of the Fall we have been considering is located within such a particular grouping, that is alongside other Old and New Testament images, such as Jonah, Moses, and Christ.[13]

In setting forth such a "scheme," however, Grabar stresses the importance of the dynamic relationships operative between particular Old and New Testament images and how this imparts meaning to the thematic whole.[14] Consequently, whatever expressionistic inconsistencies we may perceive among the catacomb paintings considered thus far would be of less import for Grabar than the overriding thematic unity that binds them together with other religious imagery to create a singular grouping.[15] For the purposes of thematic expression, and in order to facilitate the viewer's recognition, it is sufficient that such formal arrangements of Adam and Eve are consistently represented from grouping to grouping, i.e., two nude individuals, that is Adam and Eve (possibly void of any emotional content), standing astride a tree with a serpent coiled around it; and this certainly is the case in all the representations we have looked at so far.

Grabar's methodology therefore shifts the focus away from any attempt to identify expressionistic inconsistencies among individual fourth-century representations and reduces in importance any inquiry into why some representations of Adam and Eve would possess emotional content and why others would not. Why? Because in order to generate answers to these types of comparative questions would require the images to be removed from whatever *thematic* context they are located in, individually compared to one another, and the reasons for any differences sought for within the social, religious, and cultural milieu that produced them.

Given the limits of Grabar's methodology, an appeal to the particular formal qualities of the artwork itself, or its thematic context, would be unable to generate any substantive explanations regarding the catacomb painter's infusion of emotional content in room 57.[16] As to why this particular Christian artist chose to represent Adam and Eve in states of emotional distress, I would suggest, ought to be measured within his own self-understanding of what it meant to be a Christian, and his experience as a sexual being newly defined by that religion. Michel Foucault's "techniques of the self" entails a program that generates meaningful insights into the construction of such a self-identity, that is, within the limits of Christian initiation. His program challenges us, moreover, to find not only qualities unique to the individual but also the communal rites that exerted some influence over the transformation of an individual's secular identity into a Christian identity. Under the direction of certain practices guided by a "self" at war with the desires of its own body and the specific authority of a burgeoning ecclesiastical authority within the church structure, I would suggest that a new ethical being comes to the fore whose psychology, and particularly aesthetic sensibility, are shaped and limited within his or her newly discovered self. The practices and institutions I believe go the furthest in explaining the creation of this new self are third-century Christian asceticism and the third and fourth century Roman institution of mixed nude bathing.

III.

During the third century CE, Christians co-existing in Roman society responded to their growing persecutions in the form of ascetic practices. This type of Christian asceticism entailed a general prohibition against the excessive indulgence of food, erotic and sexual attractions, and the everyday pleasures of life. In short, Christian abstinence was summed up and reconstituted under the principle of "the pleasure of no pleasure."[17] Underlying and informing such ascetic maxims existed a particular understanding of the body as appropriated within a Christian context. Margaret Miles echoes the opinion of patristic fathers when she identifies the body's potential for experiencing suffering, lust, and pleasure as giving meaning to ascetic practices of denial and abstinence.[18] Such self-awareness on the part of Christian ascetics, however, did not entail an awareness beyond their own individual experience of lust. In other words, third-century

Christians did not need an ecumenical council or the opinions of patristic fathers to inform them of the obvious. Nor was it apparent that an understanding of the theological doctrine of the Fall was a pre-requisite for engaging in ascetic practices.[19] It was simply enough to identify one's body as the locus for pleasure, which in turn led to various forms of abstinence, ultimately inspiring Christian ascetics to flee to the Egyptian desert in order to "grapple alone with the demons of lust, anger, and boredom."[20]

What are we to gather from an initial understanding of third-century Christian asceticism? First, that the identity of the Christian self as well as the Christian community was *not* to be founded on the body per se, but rather on the body's potential for experiencing lust, desire, and especially pain.[21] In essence, you were Christian if, in addition to abstaining from bodily pleasures, you suffered persecution or death for your beliefs.[22] And it was through imitating the actions of Christian martyrs and ascetics who had gone before that a sense of community was founded along with other fellow Christians. Through suffering and self-denial one not only connected with living Christians, but also inherited an historical community and legacy as well. It was even said that St. Augustine owed his conversion to celibate monasticism upon hearing and reading the historical accounts of other Christians who had made the same choice.[23]

Along with the strong sense of communal and self-identity Christians acquired through the suffering body came the additional need to distinguish themselves from other groups in Roman society and in less enthusiastic ways. This process took the form of separation and exclusion from the normal everyday activities that non-Christian Romans participated in, particularly mixed-nude bathing. Apparently the issue of nakedness was of little or no consequence to a non-Christian society already inclined toward seeing nudity in art, society, and culture.[24] Familiarity with looking at nude bodies was apparent in the ever-present character of "Hellenizing" art forms that preceded the Late Antique style and commencing with Constantine.[25] Nudity attended birth and death, and was a part of gladiatorial entertainment; but most importantly, it was a part of public health, the most incessant confrontations with it being the nakedness Romans encountered in public baths.[26] While Pliny the Elder was the first to record in the first century CE the practices of mixed-nude bathing, by the fourth century it was considered a social norm limited to the middle and lower classes. Given then the extent to which nudity was a ubiquitous aspect of Roman society, we are forced to consider to what lengths Christians tolerated the practice of public nude bathing and did they offer any systematic critique of it.[27]

That the practices of mixed-nude bathing ran contrary to Christian morality was apparent in statements made to the general body of Christian males as early as the fourth century CE, specifically in the form of *Apostolic Constitutions*:

> When you walk abroad in public and wish to bathe, make use of that bath which is appropriated to men, lest, by showing your body in an unseemly manner to women, or by seeing a sight not seemly for men, either you are ensnared, or you ensnare and entice to yourself those women who easily yield to such temptations.[28]

Church statements prohibiting Christians from such public institutions as mixed-nude bath houses indicates a reactionary and systematic rejection of social norms and practices that ran counter to their own notions of morality.[29] The Christian critique of pre-existing Roman social values and institutions did require, of course, the additional assistance of church leaders and intellectuals who provided a general orthodoxy on the nature of carnal sin and temptation as already implied in the *Apostolic Constitutions*. Devising a general orthodoxy, therefore, had the two-fold effect of not only highlighting the salient features of Christian morality but distinguishing its practitioners even more as a group from among the varying religious groups and political factions existing in Rome at the time.[30] How did these general orthodox views come about, and are their origins traceable to some pre-existing social condition already mentioned?

IV.

The notion of the body as the locus of temptation for illicit sexual relations was an idea already understood among Christians at least as early as the third-century ascetic movements. But between the ever-increasing conversion rates to Christianity in the third century and its official establishment as the state religion of the Roman empire in 392 CE, church leaders sought to exert an even greater influence over the bodies of individual Christians. One avenue was through the intricate maze of personal and individual morality as related to matters of sexual relations. That the social issues of nudity and sex in Roman society warranted the attention of church authorities was evident in the number of official statements circulated on the topic. Samuel Lauechli, for instance, has analyzed the canons of the *Council of Gangra* 309 CE, and discovered that forty-six percent of the eighty-one canons issued were concerned with sexual relationships and practices.[31] Apparently even as early as 309 CE the personal and communal morality indicative of asceticism was already beginning to be supplanted by the litmus test of established canonical law. It was just a matter of time until church fathers devised a generally coherent theological understanding of the body's potential for sexual immorality, and its incitement to lust, within the context of Old Testament narratives such as the Fall of Adam and Eve. For instance, in 380 CE, St. Ambrose was to identify the results of Adam and Eve's sin, and carnal sin generally, as being located in the *shame* of recognizing their own nakedness. And St. Augustine was to later note that upon Adam and Eve's partaking of the fruit of the tree of knowledge of Good and Evil, shame was the result of the stirring of lust at the site of each other's *nakedness*.[32]

The rising rates in Christian converts and the extent to which those converts were to engage, tolerate, and reject certain aspects of Roman society were social issues allowing the church greater influence over the lives of its lay ministry. It is important to note then how the general orthodoxy and systematization of Catholic dogma, which began in the fourth century CE and continued well on into the fifth century, was due in part to certain social factors and conditions the church was contending with at the time: ever-increasing convert baptisms and the problems of coexisting in a largely non-Christian society. The religious and social milieu we find in Christian society of the fourth century can therefore be characterized as one of greater consolidation in terms of power, belief, and homogeneity in Christian living and dogma, in contrast to the "loose" and "unfocused" theology typical of the second century CE.[33] How this transition occurred was in due, in part, to the church's position on issues such as public nudity, and the extent to which its lay ministry was to resist engaging in such activities.

What we find corresponding with the distillation of a general orthodox theology, is an aesthetic transition most notably present in the remains of catacomb paintings of the fourth century CE. Artistic evidence indicates an "uneasy" transformation occurring in the representation of nudity in Christian art from the preceding second and third century CE. For instance, we find existing among earlier third century representations of Daniel, Jonah, Adam and Eve, and the resurrected in Ezekiel's vision, a freer understanding and expressive attitude toward nude representation that even non-Christian/Roman eyes would have been accustomed to seeing (see fig. 10, from Grabar, 129, *Early Christian Art*, 1968).[34] When we enter the fourth-century catacombs of Saints Marcellino and Pietro, however, a marked transition has occurred. On wall number five of room 57, we no longer perceive the classical ease in nudity we find in the earlier catacomb paintings of Old Testament personages. Heads tilted, hunched forward, and shielding their genitals, the nudity displayed by Adam and Eve has been transformed and contextualized according to Christian dogma. The stirrings of lust that plagues man in the fourth century and warns him away from the shameful expression of his own nudity in Roman public bath houses now has its etiological location in the visual representation of Adam and Eve's guilt and shame after recognizing their own nakedness.

V.

Close observations of the image in room 57[35] reveals how the artist resists, like the other paintings, representing male and female nudity according to classical principles of symmetry, balance, and proportion. This is due to many factors, of course. The associating and necessary distancing from the pagan tradition by denying its affirmation in fourth-century Christian painting was certainly one among the many important political moves. Also, the signative style, or sketchiness of form in representing human forms had a transcendent quality. Representations were meant to liberate the viewer from this world and its sensuousness, and inspire one to look beyond the superficial representation itself. To reflect on the meaning of salvation was paramount, and so to deliberately represent classical nude bodies that bewildered the eye and hypnotized the viewer through the artist's virtuosity ran counter to the Christian image functioning as a conduit to more transcendent truths.

Are the representation of shame and guilt expressed in room 57[36] wholly reducible to the social, political, and artistic discourses of the times? While typically the church's controlling technique of dominance over its early membership was exercised through the power of a general orthodoxy, the self-consciousness of the newly baptized Christian was not entirely limited to the impact of social and religious institutions in shaping that self-identity. Manifested in the catacomb painting from room 57 is a highly charged subjectivity whereby the artist reflects a personal rather than institutional bias. His own unique moniker finds expression and identification through representing an emotional idea that is not found in any other contemporary representations of Adam and Eve from the catacombs of Saints Marcellino and Pietro, perhaps because he, too, has shared the same feelings of shame and guilt felt by his first parents.

This speculation certainly goes far in explaining the formal qualities that confront the eye of a modern critic. But when construed as an art form that sacrifices form to the overriding importance of content, we seem to have gotten nowhere in "de-Medievalizing," so to speak, the commonly held belief of Early Christian art as "decline" initially addressed at the beginning of this paper. Certainly, as Ernst Kitzinger points out, it is not the case that Early Christian artists simply lacked the abilities to represent human bodies according to classical models, but, rather, that such models ceased to be meaningful or "relevant" to the fourth-century Christian.[37] They were meaningful to Ancient Greece of course, precisely because such standards of beauty warranted their production. Moreover, the Greek viewer associated the aesthetic proportionality of the human form with ethical excellence. Sex was viewed as one force among many others seeking to control the body, and was therefore something that needed to be controlled and managed, not altogether extirpated mentally and physically, as we have seen in Christian ascetic practices.[38] Represented "nudity" in Greek art is free of the shame and guilt inherent in Early Christian art precisely because happiness was the product of a measured excellence in ethical behavior, which translated itself into an aesthetic proportionality of the body and a measured poise in its gait.

Sex and nudity held a different place in the self-identity of newly baptized Christian converts, and could either be seen as something positive or negative given the context in which it was discovered, e.g., either secular or paradisiacal. For instance, in the third and fourth centuries, Christian baptisms were performed in the nude free of any and all sexually lurid connotations because the rite of baptism symbolized the emergence of a new soul accepted into a state of child-like innocence comparable to the state of Adam and Eve prior to their transgression.

Conclusion

One of the most important determining factors, I would suggest, in coming to an understanding of the disparities between Antiquity and Early Christian art is the advent of Christian self-consciousness and its being infused into artistic form. The expression of guilt and shame on the faces of Adam and Eve represent an altogether different understanding of human nudity and sexuality once the realization of a new ethical being comes to the fore. According to Michel Foucault, Christian techniques of self-realization were not those of the Greek philosopher: "that is to acquire mastership over oneself by victory of the will."[39] For the Christian, self-realization was acquired by perpetually controlling one's thoughts, "to discover the truth in oneself and defeat the illusions and images that are continuously produced in the mind by Satan."[40] Hence, sexual ethics moves beyond the relations of people and the penetration model of Antiquity to the problem of how one relates to oneself and the problem of erection. Augustinian theology explains the resulting excitation of the penis to erection beyond the control of man to be the defining image of man as "rebel."[41] Man's shame subsequent to Adam's partaking of the fruit is not due to the simple awareness of his bare and exposed genitals, but the discovery that his sexual organs, subsequent to eating the fruit, are now moving without his consent.[42] The catacomb fresco that depicts Adam and Eve possessed of shame and guilt is therefore expressive of a highly nuanced shift in the meaning of nudity and human sexuality in the history of art. Via Foucault's technique of the self, the goal of the Christian convert is not merely to control behavior, but also to control the stream of thoughts that bombard human consciousness and cause the body to disobey the will of man. Accordingly, the initiate's discovery of the attendant shame that follows such disobedience redeems Early Christian art from decline through a new sense of self-identity informing the aesthetic imagination of the Early Christian artist.

OHIO UNIVERSITY

NOTES

[1] See Fig. 1, from Jas Elsner, Imperial Rome and Christian Triumph (Oxford: Oxford UP, 1998), 16.

[2] See Fig. 2, from Elsner, 62. The term "Late Antiquity" refers to that transitional period in the history of art where newwinnocatoin in style and form were set into by the "collapse of the classical Greek canon of forms" (Ernst Kitzinger, *Byzantine Art in the Making.* (Cambridge: Harvard UP, 1968), 7). Several strains of artistic styles fall under their general rubric of "Late Antique," such as Earl y Christian art, Plebian art, or sub-antique art etc., and even though some of those styles are united in their rejection of the classical Greek canon, their subjects nevertheless do vary. Often times I will speak of Early Christian art under the broader rubric of Late Antique.

[3] Kitzinger, 9.

[4] See Fig. 3, from Elsner, 62.

[5] See Fig. 3, from Johannes Georg Deckers, *Die Katakombe Santi Marcellino e Pietro* (Münster: Aschendorff, 1987).

[6] Deckers, 18, 29, 33, 35.

[7] See Fig. 4-6, from Deckers.

[8] See Fig. 5 and 6, from Deckers.

[9] Elsner, 223.

[10] Elsner, 223.

[11] Andre Grabar, *Christian Iconography* (Princeton: Princeton UP, 1968), 12.

[12] Grabar, 12-13.

[13] See Bosio Fig. 7-9, from Deckers. While some of these catacomb paintings are in deplorable condition, and hence their iconographical groupings difficult to discern, such groupings are clearly perceivable in the Bosio representations found in Deckers' *The Catacombs of Saints Marcellino and Pietro*: Tafel 39, 41.

[14] Grabar, 12, 19, 20.

[15] Grabar, 12, 19, 20.

[16] See Fig. 4, from Deckers.

[17] Quoted in Margaret R. Miles, *Plotinus on Body and Beauty* (Oxford: Blackwell, 1999), 19.

[18] Miles, *Plotinus on Body and Beauty*, 19.

[19] Certainly accounts of the Adam and Eve narrative were to be found in the *Pentateuch*. Also, Philo of Alexandria speaks at length on the subject of Adam and Eve in paradise. Interestingly, Philo mentions nothing on the topic of shame and guilt

associated with their partaking of the fruit. He discusses at length the evil, wickedness, and spiritual death Adam suffers as a result of disobedience but does not actually describe in narrative form the feeling of shame we see depicted in room 57 (cf. 67-70).

[20] Miles, *Plotinus on Body and Beauty.*

[21] Miles, *Plotinus on Body and Beauty*, 19; Judith Perkins, *The Suffering Self* (London: Routledge, 1995), 3.

[22] Miles, *Plotinus on Body and Beauty*, 18, 19.

[23] Miles, *Plotinus on Body and Beauty*, 19.

[24] Margaret R. Miles, *Carnal Knowing* (Boston: Beacon, 1989), 26.

[25] Ernst Kitzinger identifies the existence of a Hellenistic art style flourishing in Rome during the second-century AD (7).

[26] Miles, *Carnal Knowing*, 26.

[27] Miles, *Carnal Knowing*, 26.

[28] Quoted in Miles, *Carnal Knowing*, 28.

[29] Miles, *Carnal Knowing*, 28.

[30] Miles, *Carnal Knowing*, 28.

[31] Samuel Laeuchli, *Power and Sexuality* (Philadelphia: Temple UP, 1972), 89.

[32] Saint Augustine, 464-6; Miles, *Carnal Knowing*, 92.

[33] James Snyder, *Medieval Art* (New York: Harry N. Abrams, 1989), 16.

[34] Miles, *Carnal Knowing*, 26.

[35] See Fig. 4, from Deckers.

[36] See Fig. 5, from Deckers.

[37] Kitzinger, 9.

[38] Michel Foucault, "Sexuality and Solitude," *On Signs.* Ed. Marshall Blonsky (Baltimore: Johns Hopkins UP, 1985), 371.

[39] Foucault, 371.

[40] Foucault, 372.

[41] Foucault, 372.

[42] Foucault, 372-4.

Disregarding the Text:
Postmodern Medievalisms and the Readings of
John Gardner's *Grendel*

Anna Kowalcze

"We need to interpret interpretations more than to interpret things."
Montaigne

Beowulfiana[1]

One of the first (extant) comments on the contents of the poem we know as *Beowulf* states that in it *descripta videntur bella, quae Beowulfus (auidam Danus ex Regia Scydingorum stripe ortus) gessit contra Sueciae Regulos*.[2] This (non)readerly assumption, being as it is an expression of Humfrey Wanley's unfamiliarity with the work he was describing, belongs to the hoard of *Beowulf*iana: a multitude of texts extrapolating from, amplifying, or otherwise commenting on the poem. Wanley's presentiment concerning the presumable leitmotif of what in his view might legitimately be called a quasi-classical epic, is symptomatic of the operations of other *Beowulf* critics/readers, who in a usual readerly practice of decoding, recontextualizing, and reactualizing a text have used (or violated) it as a *tabula rasa* for inscribing on it their critical/readerly presuppositions. According to foundational works of Umberto Eco, such as *The Open Work* or *The Role of the Reader*, all texts are approached by their readers from a particular ideological perspective, but *Beowulf* is an interesting case of a work analysed for a long time almost exclusively in a positivist philological fashion.[3] The text itself has been, especially in the early years of *Beowulf* criticism, written *into* its dominant interpretations and, as a consequence, suppressed. This peculiar fate of a work of art repeatedly forced into an established reading and disregarded in the process is shared by the postmodern novel *Grendel*, published in 1971 by American creative writer and medievalist John Gardner. The affinity between *Beowulf* and its contemporary retelling is a result of an "operation of textual inference upon an intertextual competence"[4] and may be treated as an instance of radical intertextuality, already implied by the dichotomy of the two titles.[5] What is most significant for the purpose of this essay, however, are the transtextual strategies functioning not so much on the structural and linguistic levels (intertextuality proper), but rather related to the interpretive potential of the hypertext (*Grendel*) with regard to its hypotext (*Beowulf*). Metatextual signals identifiable in the novel place *Grendel* among other interpretations of the epic[6] and provide a *tertium comparationis* for an examination of the dialogue taking place between the novel, its reviews and analyses, and the critical commentaries on the poem. In this essay I shall draw upon this dialogue, by its very nature intertextual as well, in order to trace possible reasons for the palimpsestic readings of *Grendel* (and by extension, of *Beowulf*), which disregard the text, yet simultaneously appropriate an exclusive right to its seemingly uniform and *true* interpretations. This particular case study may serve as a short comment on the place of the contemporary literary theory in the field of medievalism and add to the vision of the Middle Ages that we continually create ourselves.

Grendel

John Gardner's first novel to attract a lasting popular appeal and an immense critical acclaim, *Grendel* may be considered a perfectly rendered reworking of the Old English epic. It elaborates on the theme of Beowulf's first fight with monsters and narrates from the original antagonist's monstrous point of view the events that took place between Grendel's first visit to Heorot (called Hart in the novel) and the moment of his death.

> The old ram stands looking down over the rockslides, stupidly triumphant. I blink. I stare in horror. "Scat!" I hiss. "Go back to your cave, go back to your cowshed – whatever." He cocks his head like an elderly, slow-witted king, considers the angles, decides to ignore me. I stamp. I hammer the ground with my fists. I hurl a skull-size stone at him. He will not budge. I shake my two hairy fists at the sky and I let out a howl so unspeakable that the water at my feet turns sudden ice and even I myself am left uneasy. But the ram stays; the season is upon it. And so begins the twelfth year of my idiotic war.
>
> The pain of it! The stupidity!
>
> "Ah, well," I sigh, and shrug, trudge back to the trees.[7]

This rather abrupt beginning *in medias res* opens near the final resolution of the plot known from the epic: the first chapter illustrates an impasse in Grendel's war with Hrothgar, not long before the arrival of Beowulf, whose name remains unknown to Grendel, and hence is never mentioned in his first person narrative. In the following chapters Grendel reminisces about his own past, in a series of flashbacks telling the story of his childhood and adolescence, filled first with the exploration of his underworld home and then, after discovering a sunken door in the pool guarded by firesnakes, with excursions into the woods spreading above his cave. Because young Grendel wanders too far one day, he falls into a crack between two old oak trees, and is attacked first by a bull (re-presenting, like the ram met one spring several years *later*, the blindness of natural instincts) and then by Hrothgar and his thanes, who deliberate on the nature of the encountered creature. They conclude that Grendel must be a fiendish spirit and decide to kill him. Though Grendel's mute mother rescues her son, he is already lost: Grendel's solipsism formed as an act of defiance against the deterministic universe[8] ("I alone exist"[9]) is shaken by this first confrontation with men, "thinking creatures, pattern makers … [that] create universe blink by blink."[10] He finds an alluring affinity between men and himself, even if their violence and belligerence seem absurd to him. Season after season Grendel observes Hrothgar carve his kingdom in bedlam of bloodshed and plunder until a blind man with a harp approaches the king's barbaric hall. The scop begins to chant an entrancing song glorifying the deeds of Scyld and drawing a parallel between them and the achievements of Hrothgar, elevated in the lay. The beauty of the vision captivates Grendel, and yet he cannot understand the contradiction between the truth of the events he witnessed and the truth created by the harper's art:

> I … crept away, my mind aswim in ringing phrases, magnificent, golden, and all of them, incredibly, lies.
>
> What was he? The man had changed the world, had torn up the past by its thick, gnarled roots and had transmuted it, and they, who know the truth, remembered it his way – and so did I … I knew the truth. *It was late spring. Every sheep and goat had its wobbly twins. A man said, "I'll steal their gold and burn their meadhall!" and another man said, "Do it now!"*
>
> … Yet I also remembered, as if it had happened, the great Scyld, of whose kingdom no trace remained, and his farsighted son, of whose greater kingdom no trace remained. And the stars overhead were alive with the promise of Hrothgar's vast power, his universal peace.[11]

The most significant moment in Grendel's story comes when Hrothgar, inspired by the creative power of the Shaper's songs, builds Hart, "a magnificent meadhall … to stand forever as a sign of the glory and justice of Hrothgar's Danes."[12] At a feast celebrating the completion of the hall the Shaper recites the Creation Song, while Grendel, who started to believe in poetry's potential to transmute human hearts, approaches the warrior circle and stumbles over a disfigured body of a robbed man. Hearing that he himself comes from "the terrible race God cursed,"[13] he runs into the open still holding the dead body and pleads mercy and peace. He defends himself against warriors, who do not pay heed to his pleas, and flees into the woods only to come back two days later and listen to the Shaper's inaccurate account of what had happened. Moved and simultaneously infuriated by the distorted vision presented in poetry Grendel deliberates on the veracity of the songs, but soon he is lured by his new mentor, "serpent to the core,"[14] the dragon, who envisages a universe governed by entropy and rejects the Shaper's myths as illusion of reality. He states, however, that men need Grendel as the "brute existent by which they learn to define themselves."[15] After the conversation with the cynical materialist, Grendel discovers that the dragon made him invulnerable to human blows, but he soon becomes bored with war, and seeks amusement playing cat and mouse with Unferth, the Danish champion, who truly belongs to "the terrible race"[16] of Cain, since he had killed his brothers in anger. Unferth repeatedly spouts heroic lines and wishes to die an honourable death that is refused him by Grendel: the monster first pummels the unfortunate warrior with apples and then, when the flawed hero follows him to his underwater cave and falls asleep with fatigue, deposits him unhurt at the gate of the hall. Humiliated, Unferth persists with his attempts and turns into a pitiable figure refusing to renounce his "inner heroism,"[17] and seeking redemption for past sins, till the moment when Hrothgar's newly wedded wife, Wealtheow, forgives him in a truly queenly fashion. Grendel is lured by her beauty and grace, which appease conflicts in the meadhall and add to the symbolic meaning of Hart, as created by the Shaper, and then re-created by Hrothgar, but he also strongly resents her: "How many times must a creature be dragged down the same ridiculous road? The shaper's lies, the hero's self-delusion, now this: the idea of a queen!"[18] Accordingly, he exposes her as nothing but flesh, and thinks he has denied everything that the Shaper, Unferth, and Wealtheow represent. Still, the ultimate manifestation of the mythic "pattern-making" awaits him: the struggle with the heroic ethos incarnated, Beowulf, whose arrival he espies with ecstatic uneasiness. Grendel is baffled by the danger he senses in the person of the strange warrior and finally, in the last scene when they grapple, he panics at Beowulf's affirmation that "Time is the mind, the hand that makes (fingers on harpstrings, hero-swords, the acts, the eyes of queens). By that I kill you."[19] Grendel slips on the blood of a man he has just killed and has his arm torn off. In the last act of defiance the monster insists on a "mere logic of chance"[20] as the sole reason for his imminent death, but he still fulfills the fate he has chosen himself as the Danes' "brute existent."[21]

Gardnel

Since publication of the novel, *Grendel* has been appraised by the reviewers as "a prose poem of extraordinary beauty, complexity and virtuosity."[22] This exceptional unanimity with regard to the quality of the text does not correspond, however, with agreement about its meaning. The leading figure in a heated debate on *Grendel*'s established interpretation is obviously John Gardner, who in a bulk of interviews following the enthusiastic reception of *Grendel*, made a series of statements aiming at "a clarification" of diverse aspects of the novel, including its structure, symbolism, the role of sources and analogues, as well as its intended reading.

In a review by Digby Diehl in 1971,[23] Gardner voices his disapproval of its Anglo-Saxon values including the concept of heroism (as heroism for heroism's sake), and emphasizes *Beowulf*'s place in the epic dialogue extending from Homer to Dante (the view expressed as well in his stuffy application of Fulgentius's interpretation of Aristotelina virtues to the structure of the poem[24]). In Esquire 76, October 1971, he also states that "What *Grendel* does, is to take, one by one, the great heroic ideas of mankind since the beginning and make a case for these values by setting up alternatives in an ironic set of monster values. I hate existentialism."[25] An explication on the issue follows in conversations with Joe D. Bellamy[26] and Marshall L. Harvey.[27] Interviewed by Bellamy, Gardner states that the leitmotif of the novel is the history of "the main ideas of Western Civilization [and] various philosophical attitudes (though with Sartre in particular),"[28] ordered in "twelve chapters. They are all hooked up to astrological signs, for instance, and that gives you nice easy clues."[29] In the interview with Harvey, we find a claim that: "What happened in *Grendel* was that I got the idea of presenting the Beowulf monster as Jean-Paul Sartre, and everything that Grendel says Sartre in one mood or another has said, so that my love of Sartre kind of comes through as my love of the monsters, though monsters are still monsters – I hope."[30]

It becomes evident that in Gardner's opinion *Grendel* is essentially an anti-existentialist manifesto commenting ironically upon the Sartrean philosophy, which treats man as a lonely being set adrift in a meaningless universe, and which according to Gardner offers nothing but "ferocious self-assertion."[31] Instead, he argues in favour of Alfred N. Whitehead's idea of connectedness that concerns the sentience of all matter: a failure of Grendel, the intellectual (Sartrean) monster, to find a bond with the world is finally, and fatally, amended by Beowulf. To prove his point Gardner claims in a conversation with Gregory L. Morris that the twelve chapters correspond to twelve Aristotelian virtues,[32] outlining in this way the supposed organizing principle of the novel as a "connectedness" of the already mentioned "great heroic ideas" that oppose the existentialist "monster values."[33] Finally, while talking to Joseph Barbato in 1977, Gardner insists (with respect to his ill-famed biography of Chaucer) that he uses a medieval frame to explore the dilemmas of modern fiction, once more highlighting the significance of the duality of a contemporary content and the medieval(ized) form in his writing.

Gardner's arguments have been seized on by a number of critics, who almost verbatim followed his line of reasoning, incorporating into their essays most of the issues he mentions in the interviews. A few examples will suffice to illustrate my point. David Cowart, for instance, touches upon the theme of the critique of Anglo-Saxon heroism, and simultaneously connects it with an

investigation into the history of ideas that has been postulated as the
structuring strategy of the novel. In his *Arches and Light: The Fiction of John
Gardner*, we read that

> the author of *Grendel* surveys, in the *various ideas taken up*, the
> possibilities for optimism about the human condition, and in this
> respect the novel does not differ radically from the Ur-story, *Beowulf*.
> Projecting a fatalistic awareness of man's mortality and the mutability
> of all his glories, the *Beowulf*-poet also 'surveys' the claims of
> statecraft, familial love, heroism, and loyalty to gainsay the passing of
> all things: great men, great beauty, great nations. *Beowulf* at once
> endorses and questions the values of the society it describes; it
> glorifies the *ancient, heroic ideas* espoused by the pagan ancestors of its
> Christian audience at the same time that it reveals how little those
> ideas mean without the rationale provided by Christian faith. With
> *Grendel* the situation is exactly reversed. Where the earlier audience
> could look back on the pagan past and congratulate itself on its
> spiritual enlightenment, the modern audience looks back on a
> Christian past and laments its disillusionment. The desperate spiritual
> situation of the Scyldings *mirrors* our own.[34]

The issue of "monster values" is elaborated on by Michael Segedy and
Kenneth C. Mason, both of whom authenticate their argument with citations
from the interviews, as well as from Gardner's theoretical study, *On Moral
Fiction*, published in 1978. Segedy comments on the contemporary sources of
the novel in a comparative analysis of passages from Gardner's *Grendel,*
Camus's *The Stranger* and Sartre's *Nausea*, whereas Mason provides an
extensive critique of Grendel/Sartre's philosophy only to refute the precepts
of existentialism (as seen by Gardner) and eulogize the presumable intent of
the author. Mason concludes his laudatory essay in the following manner:

> The book makes a penetrating critique of a major modern
> philosophy, the existentialism of Jean-Paul Sartre, showing its ethical
> limitations as a model of human behavior ... The idea of making the
> pariah monster Grendel represent a Sartrean existentialist hero, and
> of *setting in opposition thereby the value systems of* Beowulf *and modern
> existentialist absurdism*, is a brilliant one.[35]

The structure and symbolism of the novel are further discussed by
Gregory Morris, who investigates the traces of Aristotelian philosophy in the
composition of *Grendel*; they also become the focal points for Susan Strehle
and Craig Stromme. Both Strehle and Stromme elaborate on the significance
of the number twelve in the movement of the novel and delve into its
astrological and philosophical implications: the twelve chapters of *Grendel*
presumably follow the numerological pattern of *Beowulf, The Canterbury Tales,*

and *The Waste Land*, reflecting the mythic rhythms of nature, the development of Grendel's philosophical attitudes, and the medieval Christian cosmology - all this in a perfect harmony with the auctorial intent.

None of the critics to whom I have referred is solitary in their practice of validating the interpretation of *Grendel* with recurrent references to Gardner's personal views and opinions. Chronically used phrases like "according to John Gardner," "in Gardner's view," "Gardner himself" occur in a bulk of articles and volumes amplifying on the text. Consequently, a claim that the auctorial perspective, which is preserved intact in the aforementioned articles, and hence permeates all the aspects of critical analysis of the novel, seems a justified inference. Thus, we may conclude that the majority of critics have upheld an exegesis of *Grendel* confirmed by John Gardner's commentaries subsequent to the publication of the book. They have basically followed the line of the auctorial reading, regarding Gardner's writing about his own work as the only gloss to *Grendel,* and analyzing the novel in terms of the idealistic program of "moral fiction" outlined by "Gardner himself" in a theoretical study of the same title. In this way Gardner's exegetes have made an extensive use of their reading history of the author's self-reflective criticism, and inscribed their readerly assumptions, stemming from the knowledge of his opinions, into the analysis of the text as such.

Grendulf

According to Roman Jakobson, ambiguity and self-reflectivity are characteristic of the aesthetic application of language. A text, being in itself a potentially infinite "network of different messages depending on different codes and working on different levels of signification,"[36] generates readings based on a certain model of readerly competence, but divorced from its ultimate meaning. Such (indeterminate, and hence ambiguous) interpretations are more often than not an outcome of what Eco calls the "ideological overcoding,"[37] an approach to a text from a personalized ideological perspective. By "ideological" I understand here a perspective in-formed by a given convention or other presuppositions, ensuing from the reading history of the *reader,* which at times may become concomitant with the reading history of the *work.* As we have seen above, the (critical) reception history of *Grendel* provides ample evidence to illustrate this argument; if we trace the reading history of *Beowulf,* we may come to similar conclusions. In the case of *Grendel,* the "ideological overcoding" depends on reader's ability (or willingness) to disambiguate and choose between the (self-) reflexive references of one text to others, working on "different levels of signification."

Let us examine briefly the multidimensional, theoretically infinite network of the text that in an act of reading undergoes a more or less violent metamorphosis, since it is "framed" to match the reader's horizon of expectations (i.e. his ideological perspective). As I have already indicated, the self-reflexive, intertextual play between *Beowulf* and *Grendel* does not halt at the linguistic or structural levels (though much of the first part of *Beowulf* is actually quoted or reported in the first person narrative of Grendel, who throughout the story cites lays sang at Hrothgar's court), but goes on to absorb all the characters of the hypotext as figures on loan,[38] functioning in the *other* reality of Grendel's world as culturally constituted, mutually referential entities. As a product of the postmodern "misreading" (in the Derridean sense) of *Beowulf*, i.e. an interpretation of and elaboration on what is implied and fragmentary in the epic, *Grendel* presents itself as a text commenting upon and absorbing the poem, becoming in this way a part of the metatextual dialogue taking place among *Beowulf*iana. Accordingly, we may say that the network of *Grendel* interweaves with both the text and the versatile analyses of *Beowulf*, pointing to the cruxes of *Beowulf* criticism as an iunctium and a point of departure for polysemous interpretations of *Beowulf*/*Grendel*. The manifold transtextual traces resulting from such an amalgamation offer, in my opinion, a potential activated or ignored in accordance with the reader's presuppositions – in the case of the auctorial view understood as a compliance with the reading suggested by "Gardner himself."

In the *editio princeps* of *Beowulf*, Grímur Jónsson Thorkelin writes that the nameless (obviously Danish) author of the epic "was an eyewitness to the exploits of kings Hrothgar, Beowulf and Hygelac, and was the eulogizer at Beowulf's funeral,"[39] which according to Thorkelin happened as early as A.D. 340, supposedly the year of the poem's composition.[40] This view corresponds with what we may find in *Grendel*: though the time of action is measured by the natural cycle of seasons and may be seen as fabulous (from the perspective of Grendel, who has forgotten, or never remembered, his actual age), Hrothgar's kingdom is developing in the factual time, providing an example of an early feudal state that is formed somewhere in "Daneland."[41] The scop, who performs his lays with the accompaniment of a harp, and whom the reader knows only as the Shaper, witnesses the deeds of Hrothgar and the attacks of Grendel, but he does not live long enough to see Beowulf's coming, not even to mention the hero's death. The Shaper's work is carried on by his assistant, who sings at the old man's funeral "of Hoc and Hildeburh and Hnaef and Hengest, how Finn's thanes fought with his wife's dear kinsmen."[42] The figures of two scops, who in a series of *separate* songs elevate and glorify the reality to win the monarch's favour (a variation of Alois Brandl's *Tendenzdichtung*, 'politically motivated writing"), bear a strong resemblance to the precepts of once fashionable *Liedertheorie* (ballad theory) suggesting a composite nature of *Beowulf* (transmitted orally) as well as its multiple authorship. At this point it must be noted that in the discussion of the date, provenance and the authorship of the poem as presented in the novel, *Grendel*'s critics have for the most part abandoned the text, completely ignoring the issue or propounding instead that "when Gardner 'demythifies' *Beowulf* by specifying the historical conditions of the sixth-century England [sic], he actually bestows density and force on the values carried by the poem but treated elliptically within it."[43] In both cases, the exclusion or distortion of textual traces serve to intensify the significance of the opposition between the "monster values" and "the great heroic ideas of mankind since the beginning,"[44] presumably embodied by the main characters of *Grendel*.

Another crux (or aporia), in which networks of *Beowulf* and *Grendel* are framed by readerly assumptions, is the mode of character re-presentation. There is no doubt that in *Grendel*, all characters retain at least some of the traits described in the poem, and acquire some of the features ascribed to them in diversified interpretations of *Beowulf*, but for the sake of brevity I will concentrate on the figures of Grendel and his heroic adversary, most significant for the movement of the novel. In the opening paragraphs Grendel speaks of himself as a "pointless, ridiculous monster crouched in the shadows, stinking of dead men, murdered children, martyred cows,"[45] but this statement is already colored by his earlier decision to serve as the "brute existent" of the Danes. His origin remains a mystery even to him: although Grendel preserves (with a variation) characteristics of the bestial, human, and demonic categories, his ability to understand human language, and vice versa, the ability of humans to understand him, implies a distant, unspecified kinship between him and Hrothgar's people. The desire for a definite origin pushes Grendel to appropriate the only role available to him in the world of man: that of a monster – a Nordic troll or a descendant of Cain, and subsequently the epitome of evil.[46] The changing nature of monsters and the reasons for their mutability (though analysed from a slightly different perspective) constitute one of the focal points of a seminal work on the poem, the first in the treasury of *Beowulf*iana to open itself to a possibility of a polysemous reading of the text. "The monsters *become* 'adversaries of God,'" writes John R.R.Tolkien in "*Beowulf*: The Monsters and the Critics," "and so *begin* to symbolize (and ultimately to *become* identified with) the powers of evil while they remain ... mortal denizens of the material world, in it and of it."[47]

A similar all-inclusive indeterminacy may be observed in the case of Grendel's opponent. Beowulf's characteristics abound in symbolic comparisons that comprise both the pagan and the Christian qualities of a hero: he is "an outsider not only among the Danes but everywhere;" has eyes "unfeeling as a snake's" and "no more beard than a fish;"[48] "his chest ... [is]

as wide as an oven. His arms ... [are] like beams ... as if the body of the stranger were a ruse, a disguise for something infinitely more terrible."[49] In the Unferth episode Beowulf speaks "with ... almost inhuman indifference except for the pale flash of fire in his eyes,"[50] while in the first and the last struggle with Grendel "he has wings. Is it possible? And yet it's true: out of his shoulders come terrible fiery wings."[51] The images of fish and a dragon or, as "Gardner implies," an archangel, are all reminiscent of the strong critical movement following Friedrich Klaeber's interpretation of Beowulf as a Christian hero or a type of Christ; yet an emphasis on Beowulf's self-composure and stout physicality may be also suggestive of Levin L. Schücking's claim that in the person of Beowulf fuse "the ideas of Christian stoicism and Germanic heroic norms."[52] The above excerpts lend themselves to still different readings ranging from interpretations in a vein of John M. Kemble, Karl Müllenhoff or John Leyerle (all treating Beowulf as a divine hero or a divinity), to a vision of a flawed hero that in his saying to Grendel, "It's coming, *my brother*,"[53] reveals and accepts the kinship with the monster, his "shadow self."[54]

It should come as no surprise that in the Gardnerian view the (self)reflective, transtextual potential encoded in the character re-presentation of *Beowulf/Grendel* is framed "according to Gardner:"

> In *Grendel* I was interested in ... the implications of Jean-Paul Sartre's philosophy ... It's philosophy which I think is essentially paranoid and loveless and faithless and egoistic ... So what I did in *Grendel*, I wanted to apply in modern settings some basic things of that poem, and one of the basic things, the essence of the poem is the tripartite soul, and the breakdown of reason, and man's desperate attempt to hang on to reason against what in the Middle Ages would have been treated as very simple: irascibility and concupiscence and the Platonic scheme. That system comes up in a disguise after disguise and it can always be modernized; it can be Vishnu, Brahma, Siva, or God the Father, God the Son, God the Holy Ghost, or ego, superego, id - it just keeps shape-shifting.[55]

The two protagonists (antagonists?) are almost exclusively read in the light of the idea of the triune soul, a leading concept in Gardner's "Fulgentius's *Expositio Vergiliana Continentia* and the Plan of *Beowulf*: Another Approach to the Poem's Style and Structure," in which Fulgentius's view of Aristotelian *arma* [virtue], *virum* [wisdom], and *primus* [sensuality] is applied in the discussion of the poem: Beowulf is "a superhuman among very strong men — a walking icon of *arma*. His wisdom and tact make him an icon of virum ... And *primus*: he leaves the outcome — the payment, good or bad — to God's judgment."[56] In keeping with Gardner's argument, Gregory L. Morris provides a comprehensive analysis of the unified divine soul (Beowulf) as opposed by the "configurations of corrupted virtue"[57] among which he places "the fouled *primus* or concupiscence of the dragon … the blighted *virum* or irrationality of Grendel"[58] and, somewhat surprisingly, "the demeaned *arma* or irascibility of Hrothgar;"[59] all three "corrupted virtues" are, in my opinion, suggestive of Grendel's character, as allegorised in the (Gardnerian) existentialist terms. The opposition of the divine and the chthonic trinity in *Beowulf/Grendel*, reappears in *The Construction of Christian Poetry in Old English*, in which Gardner follows the footsteps of Klaeber in stating that "the hero is unquestionably 'Christlike,'"[60] and draws detailed parallels between the Biblical story and the deeds of son of Ecgtheow, accentuating once again the importance of the allegorical frame of *Beowulf/Grendel*.

As rudimentary as it may be, the above analysis allows for a conclusion that the "textual inferences" offered by *Beowulf* and *Grendel* (*with*-and-*in* the indeterminacies bound to the date, provenance, authorship, as well as the characteristics of the main figures of *Beowulf/Grendel*), invite a manifold reading of both the poem and the novel. The history of *Beowulf* criticism shows that even though the network of the epic has been framed to fit theoretical demands/presuppositions of its readers/critics, the long strife for an ur-meaning inherent to the poem has been abandoned in favour of more "open" interpretations. In the Gardnerian reading of *Grendel*, however, there has been no acceptance of the polysemous meaning of the text.

The Palimpsest

The premise underlying "academic" Gardnerian criticism is an acceptance of the person of John Gardner as the residual of the ultimate meaning of the novel. Accordingly, the purpose of *Grendel* criticism has been to elaborate on the author's intention, and stigmatise as non-expert "misreadings" all the interpretations dissenting from the opinions propounded by Gardner's exegetes. We may say, once again using Eco's semiological analysis of works of art, that this assumption constitutes the totalizing ideological bias of Gardner and *his* critics, as the *readers* of the novel, and differentiates it from the "non-expert," "popular," but still diversified interpretations of *Grendel*. From the auctorial perspective, *Grendel* is a text which "seem[s] to be structured according to an inflexible project … [and which] obsessively aim[s] at arousing a precise response on the part of more or less precise empirical readers … Every step of the 'story' elicits just the expectation that its further course will satisfy."[61] In other words, in the Gardnerian view *Grendel* must be perceived as a "closed text," offering a fixed interpretation (in this case a denunciation of the existentialist philosophy from a moral standpoint reflected in an allegory of the fight between men and monsters), and assuming the existence of a non-specified textually "Model Reader," who absorbs the interpretation unchanged. In the *auctorial*[62] intent the model of the competence of *Grendel*'s reader is supposed to come exclusively from the context, in other words, from Gardner's "clarifying" commentaries as well as the hermeneutics of his followers. This, however, is an instance of a radically ideological reading that disregards the text of the novel and its polysemous potential, traceable in *Grendel* in particular and in *Beowulf*iana in general as the *all*-inclusive "textual strategy,"[63] i.e. the (inter)textual intent of the *scriptor*. Hence, ideological bias of the Garderian criticism forces the empirical reader to surgically close the novel, and interpret it in an aberrant manner, that is in accordance with Gardner's reading, but "not complying to author's [scriptor's] assumption" as manifested by the text.[64]

What then may be the "aberrant" Gardnerian presupposition? In his discussion of "private codes and ideological biases of the addressee,"[65] Eco gives as an exemplificatory aberrant reading the *medieval* interpretation of *Aeneid*, which, incidentally or not, was also used by Gardner to analyse *Beowulf/Grendel* in vein of the Fulgentian allegorizing tradition. In my opinion, the private code that influences the auctorial type of reading is an idiosyncratised vision of the Middle Ages in general and of *Beowulf* in particular that Gardner, as a reader of the novel, incorporated in his interpretation, and which, in the socially accepted process of an *authoritative* assessment of a text, affected the consecutive critical readings of *Grendel*. Per Whinther provides a brilliant illustration of my argument in his study with the telling title, *The Art of John Gardner: Instruction and Exploration*:

> There is a close correlation between Gardner's philosophical beliefs and his artistic practices ... One conscious method of exploration is for Gardner to *engage the literary tradition* ... Another equally important way in which Gardner consistently sets up his 'literary experiments' is by juxtaposing contrary ideas or principles (such as order and disorder, body and mind), watching closely to see what truths may issue from the ideational conflict.[66]

If we recall the "academic" interpretations of *Grendel* focusing on the already mentioned "careful structuring of the novel, based on the twelve signs of zodiac (elements of astrology), and the twelve Aristotelian virtues,"[67] as well as on the "ideas" embodied by Grendel and Beowulf, Hrothgar and his queen Wealtheow, in other words on the *presumable allegorical framing of the novel, which would "juxtapose contrary ideas," it is very easy to connote *Grendel* with a psychomachy, in which personifications of good and evil are involved in a struggle for a (tripartite) soul, and which, in Gardner's intent, should be treated as an universal and hence atemporal allegory. Nonetheless, still in Gardner's intent, the location of an essentially contemporary, existentialist and multi-dimensional/demential[68] character against a "primitivized" human setting, which allows for the probation of the character and a consequent exposition of his (seeming) failure, blurs the classification of *Grendel* as a historically oriented, and yet atemporal allegory. As we have already seen, the amalgamation of metatextual traces identifiable in *Grendel* enables us to interpret the figures of Grendel and Beowulf, Hrothgar and Wealtheow, Unferth and the Shaper as archetypal characters (and much more than that), "in keeping with the medieval (and fairy-tale) nature of Gardner's [sic] narrative."[69] But in *Grendel,* "there is no real interest in the historical background," nor are the characters "representative of their period."[70] The reason behind the ambivalence of the medieval context, which seems to be substantiated by the radical intertextual link with *Beowulf,* is that the auctorial interpretation, establishing the character of Grendel as a nihilist, and treating all the characters in the novel as *archetypal* exponents of post-medieval worldviews, exploits/explodes the early medieval background as, to use Eco's terminology once again, a "pretext," a framework for an expression of a particular ideological message, here the anti-existentialist manifesto. According to Eco, the Middle Ages as a "pretext" may be defined as "the mythological stage on which…contemporary characters are placed … [and on which] the fictional characters must move among 'real' historical figures who will support their credibility."[71] Although the setting of *Grendel* is "medievalized" (*vide* my analysis of the date, provenance and authorship of *Beowulf* in the network of its hypertext), and hence "mythologized," the auctorial insistence on the allegorical treatment of the novel violates the first condition for defining it as "medievalist." If we consider the other crux in the book, the question of character re-presentation, we will see that the characters are *potentially* indeterminate: they may well function on the level of the archetypal, the mythological, the early medieval (epic); yet in Gardnerian criticism they are treated first and foremost as the epitomes of *post*-medieval philosophical worldviews. What is more, the "'real,' historical figures" that function in the novel as the background "helping us to enjoy the fictional characters"[72] are not "real" at all: the pretext for writing the book, and the main source, the hypotext of *Grendel* is the vision of the Middle Ages as presented in another literary work, *Beowulf,* which itself refers to the Middle Ages as a "possible world … a cultural construct,"[73] in order to present its own ideological messages (whatever they may be). As the Anglo-Saxon myth of *Beowulf,* itself a copy of a copy, a simulacrum, is used and played with in *Grendel,* the network of the Middle Ages as re-created in the novel, may be treated not so much as a "pretext," but as a "*pre*-text," the text that may be changed, effaced at will, or disregarded at all, in other words, as a palimpsest.

Thus the "academic" reading, which aims at establishing a monadic, allegorizing interpretation of *Grendel,* itself builds a fiction upon a fiction, opening the seemingly "closed text," and providing a pretext (or an excuse) for other, more "popular" readings.

Derridel

The prevailing auctorial reading of the novel treats the book as an allegorical display of a failure of the system Grendel supposedly embraces, namely nihilism/existentialism. As we already know, however, the "(trans)textual strategy" of *Grendel* defends itself against the desire for the author as the final signified by offering possibilities of a polysemous interpretation, depending on reader's intertextual competence. Consequently, in spite of its totalizing tendencies, the palimpsestic reading of the novel, which frames (or rather erases) the network of the medieval (as a) text to fill it with Gardner's allegoresis, does not terminate the interplay of (self-)reflective references *with*-and-*in Beowulf*iana. Other interpretations of the novel, both various reviews as well as the response of non-academic readers, present a different, more sympathetic attitude towards "the intellectual monster" and support the claim "that man is more naturally kin to Cain than Abel."[74] This "popular" view is best exemplified by Peter S. Prescott's review,[75] often quoted within the corpora of the Gardnerian criticism as an instance of a non-expert "fundamental misreading."[76] The term used in the review in relation to both *Beowulf* and *Grendel* is "myth," which I consider the keyword to a non-Gardnerian (and subsequently non-allegorising and non-expert while still striving to encompass the auctorial perspective) interpretation of the novel. In my view, *Grendel* may be treated allegorically, but only because it speaks figuratively [*allēgorein*] about, to use a quote from the Derridel review, "a celebration and conservation of what we most need in one of the greatest poetic myths we have."[77]

Understood as a traditional story embodying popular beliefs or explaining a practice, belief, or natural phenomenon as a parable or an *allegory*, "myth" is translated from the Greek "mythos," which in turn denotes not only a story, but speech in general; a theme/plot (described by Northrop Frye as the mode of narrative organization), as well as a whole pattern of beliefs expressing, often symbolically, the characteristic or common attitudes in a group or culture. The more than double, even multiple role, which the term fulfils in language, reveals its ambivalence,[78] the possibility of functioning on the different yet overlapping levels of an oral production of a story that describes in an organized, structured way popular beliefs presented in a parabolical manner. Thus, "myth" "

> constitutes the element in which opposites are opposed [discontinuity
> of speech versus narrative organization inherent to writing; symbol

and allegory; common/popular beliefs and uniqueness of a story], the movement and play, by which each relates back to the other, reverses itself and passes into the other ... It] is the movement, the locus, the production of difference.[79]

The polysemy of the word and its logic of signification are representative of the multidimensional network(s) of *Beowulf* and *Grendel,* and consequently of their mutual elusive referent, the palimpsestic Middle Ages.

In a once fashionable mythical allegory of *Beowulf* by Karl Müllenhoff, the monsters represented the hostile North Sea and Beowulf was perceived as a helpful divinity; their struggle was hence to be seen as an eternal fight of two opposing elements, good and evil.[80] Müllenhoff's mythical allegory is dismissed in the Tolkien study already mentioned, who states that in *Beowulf* we find a multitude of meanings that reach beyond a single, simplifying allegorical reading and elude a single, as it would be said today, *autho*ritative interpretation: "a myth has other forms than the (now discredited) mythical allegory of nature: the sun, the seasons, the sea and such things ... For myth is alive at once and in all its parts, and dies before it can be dissected."[81] The individual attempts of many critics, trying to pinpoint the ur-meaning of the poem, are in this way reconciled, as their readings of the *themes* and the *beliefs* of the Beowulfian world become a part of a larger whole. The archetypal story of a classical warrior with a mysterious origin blends with the myth of a Scandinavian/Anglo-Saxon hero, being a "complete man" obeying the precepts of *comitatus,* or loyalty; in his single character are summed up, in a typical heroic fashion, a nation's illustrious past and the imperfect present leading the hero – and the nation – to defeat, *faege.* The diversified critical readings constitute a still created polysemous Anglo-Saxon "myth," whose unifying theme (and the condition of difference) may be, once again according to Tolkien, "man alien in a hostile world, which he cannot win while the world lasts."[82] Similarly, *Grendel* is not an allegorical nor a mythological novel, or rather it is not only an allegorical/mythological novel. Since the story is narrated from Grendel's *supra*-subjective point of view,[83] both the theme (general happiness of the human world versus the plague of monsters bringing out its decline) and hierarchical opposition of characters (eponymous hero, Beowulf, and the good king Hrothgar versus fiendish monsters) are questioned and rearranged, conforming thus to

> une stratégie générale de la deconstruction: in a traditional philosophical opposition we have not a peaceful coexistence of facing terms but a violent hierarchy. One of the terms dominates the other (axiologically, logically, etc.), occupies the commanding position. To deconstruct the opposition is above all, at a particular moment, to reverse the hierarchy.[84]

The novel exploits the fragmentariness and ambiguity of the relationship between the medievalized worlds of monsters and humans; the authoritarian superiority of the latter (as a Presence of *Beowulf*) being doubted and shattered in the "hierarchical reversal" of the point of view. *Grendel* questions the presupposition traceable in the poem, claiming that there is not much sense in the irrational belief that the monsters exist to serve as the Other, the evil, which is the direct counterpart of the natural, human heroic goodness. This interest in what has been excluded from the poem, in the world of monsters, as an Absence of *Beowulf* leads to the "displacement:" a centralization of figures rather marginal in the original story. Grendel's necessary critique of the whole body of values presented by the Shaper and the queen equates them with ideology devoid of an ur-meaning, a "material practice," which in Althusserian terms connects subjectivity (and a specific, biased perspective) with the beliefs of people, the "myth(os)." Grendel identifies the social and cultural context within which the Shaper's lays are chanted, but as he is isolated and marginalized by this society, he is also able to show the reader its essential hollowness: the reality the Shaper offers Hrothgar's people is a vision, "the heart-sucking conjuring tricks."[85] After the conversation with the dragon that "changed nothing, it changed everything,"[86] Grendel ascribes a specific meaning (a pretext) to his existence; his role is to complete the vision, to act as the Shaper's double.

In the deconstructionist terms, Grendel becomes "the nonoriginary origin" - not knowing his own past "because it was too long ago," he starts to act as the source of signification for Hrothgar and his people. Accordingly, Grendel's story becomes an attempt at *myth*icizing for the Danes their reality, the locus of which is his person humanizing their animal-like existence. Grendel allows the humans to build up a whole body of beliefs and superstitions concerning his origin and the purpose of his attacks; he experiments with their *myth*ologizing on the grounds of his actions. Thus, in a conscious creation of *Beowulf* myth, the order of causality is reversed, which once again brings us to the concept of deconstruction, relying by its very nature on the (Nietzschean) notion of cause as "produced by a metonymy or metalepsis (substitution of cause for effect)."[87]

Grendel's   conscious   act   of   re-creation/reallocation   of   the Scandinavian/Anglo-Saxon myth is based on his knowledge of human nature and Hrothgar's expectations. He tells and simultaneously experiences the story of his life and death in order to fulfil the tale (myth) related orally, and thus mythically. In this way, a "monster" transfigures himself into the fate, "the brute existent" of *his* Danes, their *Wyrd* weaving the thread of human lives while weaving the web of words. He serves as a substitute for the meaning ("the transcendental signified" as Derrida puts it), becoming a cause for both "the man at war with the hostile world, and his inevitable overthrow in time."[88]

The differences in the presentation of one story by two subjects – one a human, the other a nonhuman teller – lead Grendel to a reflection over the relationship between the teller and his tale, as well as between the tale and reality. Grendel learns that there is no re-presentation of world through language, but that language creates the world and reality, determined by the person of the teller. The human belief in the objective, real world that can be re-presented in the order of words, constitutes the rationale, creates the heroic code, the feeling of tribal unity, the categorized universe man urges for. Grendel knows perfectly well that both he and Hrothgar's subjects are "constituted by language as much as they are constituted of language."[89] As he lives in the world of linguistic relativity, he thus stands, as the logocentric King of Gods, in the position of power and authority with which he is endowed exactly because the humans do not know his name.

As it has been said above, *Beowulf*/the Shaper's song is presented in *Grendel* in the process of composition, of making a story (myth) that expresses with the use of oral medium (mythos) the attitudes and beliefs of a community (mythos). The scop creates a *myth*opoeia [*poien* 'make'], in which he, Hrothgar, Beowulf, and Grendel all believe. When Grendel starts to understand that the scop creates only a *vision* of reality, he calls both the corrupt community and the song itself a *monstrous* lie, classifying in this way *Beowulf*/the song as an example of human *myth*omania, an excessive tendency to tell lies or exaggerate. But as he decides to play the role of fate, he gives *his* people a motor for action, which in the world of the Scandinavian/Anglo-Saxon myth(os) is the pre-text for existence and truth (reality). He can grasp the hidden, self-creative potential of his words, the potential that has the power of destroying the weaver of the medievalized wor(l)d. Grendel's appropriation of the uniquely human right to speak is the condition of his mediated position in between the world of the humans and the monsters, re-presented by Beowulf and the Shaper on the one hand, and Grendel's mute (and thus devoid of the power to create a myth for herself) mother on the other. She is, in deconstructionist terms, the generalized absence, the "différance" alluding to the undecidable alteration ("aporia") between the perspectives of structure (the poem, human world) and event (the novel, Grendel's standpoint). In Derridean terms we may say that Grendel, bound both to his mother's silence and the scop's articulacy, takes his place between the indefinite and the defined, between the signified and the signifier. Oscillating in the relation to both of them, Grendel becomes the non-present meaning of one story set adrift by two different perspectives – his as the spokesman for the "monstrous" world and the scop's as the mythmaker. In this way Grendel dissects the "lie," the "mythological" human bias and "grafts" upon the song/the poem his *new*, essentially *other* meaning, functioning only in the relation to the Scandinavian/Anglo-Saxon polysemous myth. This is in accordance with the deconstructionist

> ... reversal attributing importance to the marginal ... [which] does not lead simply to the identification of a new center ... but to a subversion of the distinctions between essential and inessential, inside and outside ... This double practice of relying on the terms of an opposition in one's argument but also seeking to displace that opposition yields a specific graft that Derrida identifies in discussions of the logic of "paleonymics:" the retention of old names while grafting new meaning upon them.[90]

The human, Scandinavian/Anglo-Saxon/medieval myth(os), the Presence of *Beowulf* is not destroyed but rearranged, and in this way preserved -- even if in a different shape. As it has been said, Grendel first believes in the spoken story (myth), then denies it, but in his act of denial and de-construction of the Anglo-Saxon myth, he builds it anew to facilitate the possibility of a dialogue between the Shaper and Grendel; between *Grendel* and *Beowulf,* between the allegory and the myth, "giving everything at stake in the operations of deconstruction the chance, the force, the power of *communication.*"[91]

Fuga Semiotica

Coming back (or going forth for that matter) to the epigraph of this essay: Montaigne said that it is better to interpret interpretations rather than things. Given the intertextual functioning of the maxim and its appearance in one of the best known texts by Jacques Derrida (already quoted in my quotations from Culler and Marshall), it seems that an act of interpreting means commenting upon a text that is "already always elsewhere." Such an interpretive drift, whether we call it a différance, dissemination or "unlimited semiosis," is the modus operandi of all three models of reading mentioned in this study, none of which treats the text as an object of purely aesthetic contemplation. The first, sadly neglected model of Humfrey Wanley's (non)readerly assumption constructs a paradigm of the epic, in which the text is completely wiped out and disregarded by an ideological bias created by the classical literary convention. John Gardner's allegorizing interpretation infers from the text only as much as it needs for a confirmation of its precepts, and frames its potentially infinite network at will. Finally, my deconstructionist reading strives to decode and restructure polysemy of the intertexts, but in the process ineluctably frames the interweaving networks to match the project of deconstruction. For the first two models there is no vision of the Middle Ages, or rather it exists, but it is decrepit and powerless (like Grendel's mute mother), being mastered and suffering obliteration at the humanizing touch of Wanley's classicism and Gardner's anti-existentialism/anti-nihilism. Still, the medieval is never fully effaced, because it always leaves a feeble trace in its semiotic resistance to ideological closure (frame), and a subsequent semiotic escape. To accept the *fuga semiotica* of the past and to affirm the trace, the simulacrum, is to decode fragments of the palimpsest, preserving (or post-serving) in the act the multi-accentuality of medieval myth for which I have been struggling:

> There are ... two interpretations of interpretation, of structure, of sign, of play. The one seeks to decipher, dreams of deciphering a truth or an origin which escapes play ... The other, which is no longer turned toward the origin, affirms play and tries to pass beyond man and humanism, the name of man being the name of that being who, throughout the history of metaphysics of ontotheology – in other words, throughout his entire history – has dreamed of full presence, the reassuring foundation, the origin and the end of play.[92]

The transtextual strategy of *Grendel,* and analogously of *Beowulf,* is a play, implemented "elsewhere," "always" perpetuating itself between the "closing" and the "opening" of the text by its readers, because it is "already" behind in time, hidden under yet another tissue of the multi-layered and fragmented visions of the post-modern Middle Ages.

JAGIELLONIAN UNIVERSITY

NOTES

[1] I am greatly indebted to Dr. Thomas A. Shippey, St. Louis University, and Dr. Richard Utz, University of Northern Iowa, for their invaluable suggestions and encouragement, without which this essay would not take the present shape.

[2] "are seen described the wars which Beowulf (a certain sprung from the royal stock of the Scyldings) waged against the petty kings of Sweden" (quoted in T.A. Shippey, trans. *Beowulf* (London: Edward Arnold, 1978), 7).

[3] For an elaboration of the methodology of the early Anglo-Saxon studies, which I find analogous with the convictions held by the proponents of the Gardnerian criticism, see the already classical position of A. Frantzen's *Desire for Origins: New Language, Old English, and Teaching the Tradition* (Piscataway, NJ: Rutgers UP, 1991). Here I quote passages most relevant for the discussion above.

"Traditional Anglo-Saxon studies, engaged in what I have called 'the history of the document,' defer discussion of these and other equally important matters [response of all readers], assuming instead that the 'meaning' of the text is arrested at the stage of consciousness we assign to its author or original audience" (100).

"Anglo-Saxon studies are idealist in that they entertain the image of progress that idealizes and celebrates change as improvement. Objectivism allows Anglo-Saxonists to believe that their methods of analysis are conducted independent of arbitrary judgment because they appear to be highly disciplined, scientifically proven, and reliable, if not entirely error-free ... As Anglo-Saxon studies construct meaning along procedural and methodological lines, that effectively conceal ideological bias and present the 'terrain of conceptuality' ... as uncontested and regulated by 'scientific' rather than 'political' principles" (105).

[4] Umberto Eco, *The Role of the Reader: Explorations in the Semiotics of Texts* (Bloomington: Indiana UP, 1979), 4.

[5] In my discussion of intertextual relationships I follow G. Genette taxonomy (*Palimpsestes. La literature au second degree,* Paris, 1982) as modified by M. Głowiński and Ryszard Nycz. Gennete's differentiation between intertextuality and hypertextuality is liquidated as overlapping: hypertextuality is treated as a subcategory of intertextuality. The category of paratextuality is tentatively subsumed by metatextuality, whereas architextuality remains unchanged.

[6] Throughout the essay I use the term in both its meanings: the traditional one (indicating a long narrative poem recounting heroic deeds), and the etymological (Greek "epos" designating "word," "speech," "poem") in order to reflect in this way the polysemous nature of *Beowulf.*

[7] John Champlin Gardner, *Grendel* (New York: Vintage, 1989), 5-6.

[8] A more detailed analysis of the theme of the mechanized universe in Gardner's oeuvre may be found in Rudy S. Spraycar's "Mechanism and Medievalism in John Gardner's *Grendel,*" *Science Fiction Dialogues,* ed. Gary Wolfe.

[9] Gardner, *Grendel,* 22.

[10] Gardner, *Grendel,* 27.

[11] Gardner, *Grendel,* 43-4; emphasis original.

[12] Gardner, *Grendel,* 47.

[13] Gardner, *Grendel,* 51.

[14] Gardner, *Grendel,* 61.

[15] Gardner, *Grendel,* 73.

[16] Gardner, *Grendel,* 51.

[17] Gardner, *Grendel,* 88.

[18] Gardner, *Grendel,* 108.

[19] Gardner, *Grendel,* 170.

[20] Gardner, *Grendel,* 173.

[21] Gardner, *Grendel,* 73.

[22] Ruth Leslie Brown. Rev. of Grendel, by John Ch. Gardner. *Saturday Review* 2 Oct 1971: 54.

[23] "Medievalist in Illinois Ozarks." *Times Calendar* 5 Sept 1971: 43.

[24] "In *Beowulf* ... the Fulgentian scheme of the *Aneid* reappears intact, with one very important exception: the ending is tragic. But *Beowulf*-poet, influenced by Germanic and Christian ideas of the dreadful transience of things, carries his poem beyond the hero's moment of *felicitas* to an ambiguous victory and defeat" (Gardner qtd. in Gregory L. Morris, *A World of Order and Light: The Fiction of John Gardner* (Athens: U of Georgia P, 1984).

25 Qtd. in Helen B. Ellis and Warren U. Ober, "*Grendel* and Blake: The Contraries of Existence." *John Gardner: Critical Perspectives*. Ed. Robert A. Morace and Kathryn Van Spanckern (Carbondale: Illinois UP, 1982), 47.

26 Joe David Bellamy, *The New Fiction: Interviews with Innovative American Writers* (Urbana: U of Illinois P, 1974), 169-93.

27 Marshall L. Harvey, "Where Philosophy and Fiction Meet: An Interview with John Gardner," *Chicago Review* Spring 1978: 29.

28 Bellamy, 173.

29 Bellamy, 174.

30 Harvey, 75.

31 John Champlin Gardner, *On Moral Fiction* (New York: Knopf, 1973), 387.

32 Morris, 235.

33 The idea is commonsensically commented by Gregory Morris, who cannot see it as a major organizational point of the story, since it is rather difficult to distinguish in the *Nichomachean Ethics* exactly twelve virtues (235).

34 Cowart, 43-4; emphasis added.

35 Mason, 109; emphasis added.

36 Eco, *Reader*, 5

37 Eco, *Reader*, 14.

38   Theodore Ziolkowski's taxonomy in his *Varieties of Literary Thematics* (Princeton: Princeton UP, 1983), in the chapter, "Figures on Loan: The Boundaries of Literature and Life.".

39 Quoted in *A Beowulf Handbook*. Ed. Robert E. Bjork and John E. Niles (Exeter: U of Exeter P, 1998), 17.

40 If not indicated otherwise, all references to *Beowulf* criticism come from Robert E. Bjork and John E. Niles's *A* Beowulf *Handbook.*

41 Gardner, *Grendel,* 153.

42 Gardner, *Grendel,* 147.

43 Peggy A. Knapp, "Alienated Majesty: Grendel and its Pretexts," *Centennial Review* 32.1 (Winter 1988): 5.

44 Gardner quoted in Ellis and Ober, 47.

45 Gardner, *Grendel,* 6.

46 *A Beowulf Handbook*, 286.

47 J.R.R. Tolkien, "Monsters and Critics," *An Anthology of Beowulf Criticism*. Ed. L.E. Nicholson (Notre Dame: U of Notre Dame P), 69; emphasis added.

48 Gardner, *Grendel,* 154.

49 Gardner, *Grendel,* 155.

50 Gardner, *Grendel,* 162.

51 Gardner, *Grendel,* 169.

52 *A Beowulf Handbook*, 271.

53 Gardner, *Grendel,* 170; emphasis added.

54 *A Beowulf Handbook*, 222.

55 Quoted in Morris, 55.

[56] John Champlin Gardner, "Fulgentius's *Expositio Vergiliana Continentia* and the Plan of *Beowulf:* Another Approach to the Poem's Style and Structures," *Papers on Language and Literature* 6 (1970): 227-62.

[57] Morris, 55.

[58] Morris, 56.

[59] Morris, 55.

[60] Quoted in Cowart, 44.

[61] Eco, *Reader*, 8.

[62] See Barthes' Elaboration on the notion of *auctor* (originator) vs *scriptor* (entity inherent to the text understood as the process/the act of writing) in his seminal „The death of the author."

[63] Eco, *Reader*, 10.

[64] Eco, *Reader*, 22.

[65] Eco, *Reader*, 6.

[66] Per Winther, *The Art of John Gardner: Instruction and Exploration* (Albany: SUNY P, 1992), 6-7.

[67] Leonard Butts, *The Novels of John Gardner: Making Life, Art as a Moral Process* (Baton Rouge: Louisiana State UP, 1988), 87.

[68] I am obliged to Dr R. Utz for pointing out the play of words here.

[69] Butts, 94.

[70] Umberto Eco, *Travels in Hyper-Reality: Essays.* Trans. William Weaver (San Diego: Harcourt Brace Jovanovich, 1989), 68.

[71] Eco, *Travels*, 68.

[72] Eco, *Travels*, 69.

[73] Eco, *Reader*, 222.

[74] Timothy Foote, "The Great Generation," *Time* (20 Sept 1971): 89.

[75] Paradoxically, this notorious review is cited on the covers of both the English editions as well as the Polish translation of *Grendel.*

[76] Mason, 101.

[77] Quoted on *Grendel*'s cover.

[78] In accordance with Paul de Man's definition of deconstruction as "always having for its target to reveal the existence of hidden articulations and fragmentations within assumedly monadic totalities" (de Man qtd. in Culler 247).

[79] Derrida quoted in John Culler, *On Deconstruction: Theory and Criticism After Structuralism* (Ithaca: Cornell UP, 1982), 143.

[80] Niles, 218.

[81] Tolkien, 63-4.

[82] Tolkien, 78.

[83] *Supra*-subjective because Grendel is fully aware of the fact that he may approach the story of his life only through his own (sub)consciousness, and effactually determines to transgress the totality of a stable and consciously adopted standpoint.

[84] Derrida quoted in Culler, 85.

[85] Gardner, *Grendel*, 80.

[86] Gardner, *Grendel*, 73.

[87] Culler, 86-7.

[88] Tolkien quoted in K. Sisam, *The Structure of Beowulf* (Oxford: Oxford UP, 1965), 20.

[89] Foucault quoted in Brenda K. Marshall, *Teaching the Postmodern: Fiction and Theory* (New York: Routledge, 1992), 55.

[90] Culler, 140.

[91] Derrida quoted in Culler, 141; emphasis original.

[92] Derrida quoted in Marshall, 69.

"Une guerre sainte contre l'Académisme":
Louis Courajod, the Louvre, and the Barbaric Middle Ages

Laura Morowitz

In 1896, M. Kaempfen, Director of the Musées Nationaux, delivered a passionate eulogy at the funeral of Louis Courajod, whose death dealt a serious blow to the community of medieval scholars.[1] Courajod's lifework, claimed the scholar André Michel, has been "a holy war against Academism."[2] Although the writings of Louis Courajod have largely been lost to history, he was the only medievalist of the late nineteenth century to rival the popularity and importance of Emile Mâle. In fact, it was Courajod who was almost single-handedly responsible for the opening of the Département of Medieval and Renaissance Sculpture in the Musée de Louvre in 1893, bringing medieval works to the attention of a far greater public.[3]

In contrast to Emile Mâle, who argued for the Roman roots of Western medieval art, Courajod insisted in all of his writings and lectures on the "barbaric" and "Eastern" roots of Gothic art. According to Courajod, the "crude" and "popular" nature of Gothic art had been obscured and contested in the Ancien Régime and continued to be so by the bureaucratic artistic institutions of the Third Republic. It was only by uncovering and restoring the barbaric, Christian elements of Gothic art that the French nation could rightly honor her past. To approach this past ignorantly, Courajod insisted, was an "unpatriotic act."[4]

In the following paper, I examine the writings and ideas of Louis Courajod, largely through a series of lectures he delivered at the Ecole du Louvre in the early 1890's.[5] In addition, I trace Courajod's passionate commitment to establishing a medieval department in the Louvre museum, revealing the methods of display and acquisitions in the early stages of the collection. What emerges is a fascinating clash between the "scientific," "objective" display within the Louvre, and the highly subjective, "popular" rhetoric of Courajod's writings.

In 1893, the Louvre inaugurated a new wing devoted to sculptures and *objets d'art* of the Medieval and Renaissance periods. The existence of this new wing was owed largely to the efforts of one man, the pioneering medievalist Louis Courajod. Coming up through the ranks of the museum, where he served in various curatorial posts, Courajod taught a generation of students at the Ecole de Louvre.[6] Writing in a style at once lucid and polemical, Courajod took it upon himself to re-interpret the history of Gothic art. Believing the Academy and "aristocratic" forces had conspired to rid Gothic art of its savage and authentic elements, Courajod was determined to bring them back to light. He tirelessly argued for an understanding of medieval works as the product of a popular, communal art which arose directly from the masses, an interpretation which dovetailed nicely with Courajod's own leftist and nationalist leanings.

Courajod had several theses which he pursued throughout his writings and lectures. The most repeated was his insistence that Gothic art was essentially a barbaric art, one deeply influenced by Eastern and Germanic culture, rather than one that had developed organically out of late Roman elements. From the start, medieval art, born of the barbarian, Celtic tribes, was "...le fils de la période barbare."[7]

> The art of the Gauls, like the blood of the Gauls, without ever drying up, mixed and assimilated barbaric blood in certain regions destined by superior will to become the heart of a renewed and rejuvenated nationality.[8]

Moreover, it was not to the Mediterranean that the French needed to look for the roots of their "true" culture, but rather to the Christian East:

> Archaeology shows that Gaul owes nothing to the Greek colonies besides coinage and the alphabet ... The source of light had been, for us, neither Greece nor Italy, but the Black Sea, and further back, Persia and Assyria ...[9]

Accordingly, for Courajod, the French Celts, settled in Gaul, were themselves a people with ties to both East and West, who maintained their culture despite the Roman invasions. It was the unique blend of indigenous Celtic elements and Christian iconography that had given birth to French medieval art. "I will show," claimed Courajod in his lecture on "Les Sarcophages du Sud-Ouest," that from the first moments of its birth French art was born Christian ..."[10] Celtic imagination, mixed with Eastern Christian symbolism, had sown the seeds of Gothic art.[11]

Within these contentions lay Courajod's second important thesis: his assertion that "classical" or Roman culture had been nothing but dangerous and stultifying for French art.[12] In his diatribe against Roman art, Courajod portrayed it as an invader to French soil that had never succeeded in winning over the masses. "The product of a violent imposition, a military invasion,"[13] Roman art was cold and sterile, an art of "functionaries" who had conspired with the Gallic aristocracy against the masses. While medieval art had always remained "a popular art ... even in the most aristocratic period,"[14] Roman art had squelched the "democratic" spirit of the native Celtic populations.[15] Courajod went even further, giving his argument contemporary relevance by casting the modern Academy as the modern day successor to Rome, a body producing art by and for an "elite" establishment: "Roman art remained profoundly foreign to the popular masses, as distant, surely, as it is today to some of our arts cultivated in the hothouses of certain worldly or Academic milieus."[16]

Courajod drew an explicit parallel between the stultifying imposition of Roman art on the Gaulic tribes, and the stronghold of Academic style on the art of his own generation. Such parallel was underlined by his opening lecture in 1895 on "Les origines de l'art moderne: L'école académique."[17] Beginning in the seventeenth century, Courajod argued, the moribund teaching of the French Academy had cast a pallor over French art, stripping it of its life force. Four years prior, Courajod had warned contemporary French audiences that the continuing hegemony of the French Academy would succeed in destroying French art for the second time:

> We possess an art accessible to an international elite of initiated "Latins," an art which is timeless, and without nation, and which scoffs at satisfying the needs of its time and the exigencies of its natural climate, an art which requires a special training in order to be understood ... Must we surrender for the second time the soul of our country to Rome, we the elite, we the intellectual aristocracy of France, following in the footsteps of the shameful Gallic aristocracy of the Gallo-Roman period? The future will not forgive us for it. If the art of the Middle Ages had not existed, it would have been necessary to invent it, since it was, as I have shown you every day, the true expression of the temperament of the country after the mixing of the races.[18]

For Courajod, as for so many medievalists of his generation, the revival of French art would begin only under a new (and for Courajod, more leftist) political era. As he saw it, the vigor and communal force of medieval art could only be resuscitated under a socialist regime:

> The Socialists, who tomorrow will be numerous and strong are nearly absent today in the consuls of government, and in the Academies of painting. They do not participate in the established direction of the Beaux-Arts, nor in that of the Manufactures nationals.[19]

Only when the masses, the working classes, had (re)-gained power could a truly popular art bloom again.

One of Courajod's key weapons in salvaging the real history of French medieval art were his forceful lectures; another was his tireless campaign to establish a permanent collection of the full range of medieval art in the most lauded of French museums, the Musée de Louvre. Courajod's efforts were finally vindicated in 1893, when the Département de la sculpture du moyen âge et de la Renaissance was inaugurated. On the occasion of the new opening, Courajod published his *Histoire du département de la sculpture modern au Musée du Louvre*, in which he chronicled the pre-history of the new sculpture wing.[20] He traced its formation to the 1850's, citing the correspondence between the directeur général and the Minister of Culture. On 29 October 1850, Léon Laborde called for perseverance in the creation of a special Musée de sculpture du moyen âge et de la Renaissance, despite previous lack of enthusiasm for such a project.[21] As Courajod noted, the public had been slow to recognize the national treasure of the medieval age: "The taste and fashion of the day would still seem to allow the medieval and Renaissance periods to be appreciated only for their *bimbeloterie*. We cannot avoid mentioning the sudden decline in public sentiment."[22] To counter this phenomenon, the directeur general had requested the "complete and chronological organization of art history from the medieval and Renaissance periods," the "most interesting period for French art."[23] With this call the collection began in earnest, characterized by a "judicious spirit of scientific classification."[24] In a spirit of scholarly rigor, Courajod and his predecessors expanded and attempted to "complete" the existing monuments in the Louvre (derived mostly from the Royal collections, the École des Beaux-Arts, and certain pieces from Alexandre Lenoir's Musée des Monuments Français which found their way into the museum).[25] In his zeal, Courajod collected well over one thousand pieces, from many thirteenth-century standing Madonnas, to fragments of architectural capitals, to large-scale tombs.[26]

In contrast to earlier medieval public collections, including the Musée de Monuments Français, and the Musée de Cluny, the motivation behind the collection was thus no longer pleasure or an attempt to escape into the Romantic past, but primarily a didactic one.[27] Such educative purpose not only characterized the general aim of almost all museums established under the Third Republic,[28] but would serve to wrest the collection of medieval antiquities from the hands of fashionable dealers and from the art trade. Hence Courajod's pointed barb against the *bimbeloterie* of medieval works, their use as decorative devices in the homes of wealthy collectors. Moreover, for Courajod, the Romantic-based sensibility of museums like that of Cluny, which had begun life as the private collection of Alexandre du Sommerard, must have still smacked of the "aristocratic" and Royalist Middle Ages that Courajod had come so firmly to contest. Instead, the medieval collection of the Louvre (not unlike the Musée de sculpture comparée au Palais du Trocadéro, established a decade earlier in 1882) would be rigorous, objective, and "democratic" in its attempt to include the full range of styles and sub-periods and decidedly lacking in the playful and eccentric flavor of the *wunderkammer* of the rooms of Cluny.

Thus, despite Courajod's unexpected death in 1896, by the first decade of the twentieth century the collection had blossomed into a real department, arranged in a roughly "chronological" and "scientific" (if hardly "complete") manner.[29] The ground floor alongside the Court of the Old Louvre was now given over to sculpture, with the medieval and Renaissance pieces located in five rooms along the Seine, near the Pont des Arts.[30] The focus of the collection was on Royal portraiture and tombs. In room 55, the visitor encountered works from the twelfth through the fourteenth centuries, including architectural fragments as well as a *Christ Crucified* and *Seated Virgin*. This led into room 56, which held numerous Virgins of the sixteenth century as well as the greatly treasured portraits of Charles V and his wife Jeanne de Bourbon. A fifteenth-century doorway led to room 57, containing Gothic fragments, including ruins of sculpture from Notre-Dame de Paris. Statues and *gisant* tombs (such as the one of King Phillip VI of Valois, by AndréBeauneveu, and the tomb of Philippe Pot {1494}) were displayed in room 58. The final room, 59, displayed "Gothic" statuary by Michael Colombe alongside Renaissance marbles. The strict isolation of sculptured works from medieval pieces in other media contrasted sharply with the more "romantic" and "tableau vivant" display at Cluny. To glimpse French *primitif* painting, for example, the visitor to the Louvre would have had to cross over to room "L" of the Grand Gallery of paintings, leaving behind the sculpture wing.

Despite Courajod's rage against the dry bureaucratic model of the Academy and the Republican art establishment, the Louvre collection which he helped to found participated very much in the positivist and "objective" mode of the late nineteenth century institutions. Ironically, while Courajod championed a "popular and communal" art of the Middle Ages, the setting of his scholarship was perhaps the most erudite and least "popular" of all the displays of medieval art in the *fin de siècle*. While retrospectives of medieval art held at the Expositions Universelles, as well as earlier established medieval museums like Cluny, had attracted the broad public by integrating the medieval objects into period rooms or alongside contemporary works, at the Louvre, viewers were offered little to popularize the study of medieval art or to foster the kind of theatrical display that the public had come to demand. Within the sterile walls of the museum, divorced from the furniture, objects, and other works of art that originally surrounded them, the Gothic sculptures became mere objects, no longer capable of resurrecting an entire sensibility. Ironic, too, that the collection was housed in the former palace of the Louvre, perhaps the best symbol to date of the taste of the Ancien Régime, and an incontestable reminder of the establishment of the French Academy, against which Courajod turned such ire.

But perhaps the richest irony of all is one that Courajod could not have foreseen; after more than a century, the medieval works in the Musée du Louvre belong once again to the masses, to the crowds who stand in line to see them, or who study them at home with the help of the museum website. For Courajod, who insisted on the worth of "barbaric" art, we barbarians are indeed still at the gate, waving tickets rather than swords, in a place where art does, indeed, belong to everyone.

WAGNER COLLEGE

NOTES

[1] M. Kaempfen, *Funérailles de M. Louis Courajod* (Ecole de Chartres, 1896).

[2] "Une guerre sainte contre l'académisme." See André Michel, intro to Louis Courajod, *Leçons prefesees a l'École du Louvre (1887-1896)* (Paris: 1899), vol. 3, xiii.

[3] For biographical information on Courajod see Michel. Also see the pages on Courajod in Frances Haskell, *History and Its Image: Art and the Interpretation of the Past* (New Haven: Yale UP, 1993), 442-444.

[4] Courajod quoted in Kaempfen.

[5] Upon Courajod's death, the lectures which Courajod delivered from 1887-1896 were compiled in three volumes and introduced by André Michel. See above, endnote 1.

[6] In March of 1874, at the age of thirty-four, Courajod was named assistant curator of sculpture and *objets d'art* of the Medieval and Renaissance periods at the Louvre. Five years later he was promoted to curator.

[7] Courajod, "L'art byzantin," (11 Mars 1891), *Leçons*, 165.

[8] "L'art gaulois, comme le sang gaulois, sans jamir tarir, s'amagama et s'assimila le sang barbare dans certaines contrées destinées par des volontés superièures à devenir la coeur d'une nationalité renouvelée et rejeunie." Courajod, "L'élément Celtique ou Gaulois," *Leçons* 17 and 24 (Dec. 1890), 46.

[9] "L'archéologie démontre que la Gaule n'a rien dû aux colonies grecques de la Méditerranée en dehors de la monnaie et de l'alphabet... Le foyer de lumière a été, pour nous, non la Grèce ou l'Italie, mais le fond de la mer Noire, et dans le lointain, le Perse et l'Assyrie." Courajod, "Les origins de l'art gothique" Leçon d'oeuverture au cours d'histoire de la sculpture française (10 Dec. 1890). Reprinted in *Bulletin Monumental* 57 (1891-2), 47.

[10] "...je vous monterai qu'aux premières heures de sa naissance, l'art français, que est né chrétiem, n'eût de contact qu'avec la Judée, la Syrie, la Grèce, Byzance et Ravenne, c'est-à-dire avec l'orient hellenisé." Courajod, "Les sarcophages du sud-ouest," *Leçons*, (18 Feb. 1891), 109.

[11] "Tout semble indiquer que l'Orient a contribué pour une large part à la formation de l'art nouveau." Courajod, "Les origines de l'art gothique," 67. Also see "L'art barbare."

[12] Courajod, "Les origines de l'art gothique;" Courajod, "L'élément Gallo-Romain," *Leçons* 7 and 14 (Jan. 1891).

[13] "Il [Roman art] était resté partout le produit d'une importation violente, d'une intrusion militaire." "Les origines de l'art gothique," 47.

[14] "L'art du moyen-âge, issue des instincts barbares, fut un art populaire, ce qui ne l'empêcha pas d'être à la fois très raffiné et compris de tous, même dans la periode la plus aristocratique," "L'art barbare," 215.

[15] German barbarians had liberated Celtic art. "L'art barbare," 158.

[16] "Les masses populaires, restèrent profondément étrangères à l'art romain, aussi étrangères sans doute qu'elles les sont aujourd'hui à certains de nos arts cultivés en serre chaud dans certains milieux mondains ou académiques." "L'élément celtique ou Gaulois," 76.

[17] Courajod, "Les origines de l'art moderne: L'école académique," *Origines de l'art moderne* (Paris: Alphonse Picard et Fils, editeurs, 1903).

[18] "Nous possédons un art accessible à une élite internationale d'initiées latins, un art qui s'applique à n'avoir ni âge, ni patrie, et qui dédaigne de satisfaire les besoins de son temps et les exigencies du climat natal, un art qui pour être compris exige toute une culture spéciale... Devons-nous livrer une seconde fois à Rome l'âme de notre-pays, nous l'élite, nous l'aristocratie intellectuelle de la France, imitant en cela la coupable aristocratic gauloise des temps Gallo-Romains? L'avenir ne nous le pardonnerait pas. Si l'art du moyen âge n'existait pas, il faudrait l'inventer, puisque'il a été, comme je vous le montre chaque jour, l'expression sincère du tempérament de la patrie après le mélange des races." "L'art barbare," 237.

[19] "Les socialistes qui demain seront le nombre et la force, ne sont presque rien aujourd'hui dans les conseils du gouvernement, ni dans le académies de peinture. Ils ne participent pas à le direction effective des Beaux-Arts, ni à celles des Manufactures nationals." Courajod, "Influences sociales et réligieuses." *Leçons* (24 Feb. 1892), 352.

[20] Louis Courajod, *Histoire du département de la sculpture moderne au Musée du Louvre* (Paris: Ernst Leroux, 1894).

[21] "La formation d'un musée de sculpture du moyen âge et de la Renaissance exige de revendications qui, pour n'être pas toutes couronnées de succès n'en doivent pas moins se continuer avec persévérance, parce qu'elles seront approuvées quand on verra, par l'ensemble de la nouvelle collection ce qu'elles ont produits." Letter of 29 October 1850 from Léon Laborde to le Directur générale, quoted in Courajod, *Histoire*, 189.

[22] "Le goût du jour et la mode semblaient ne vouloir encore accepter, du moyen âge et de la Renaissance, que la bimbeloterie. Nous ne pouvons nous empêcher de remarquer la subit abaissement du sentiment public." Courajod, *Histoire*, 239.

[23] "... l'organization complète et chronologique de l'histoire de l'art pendant la période du moyen âge et de la Renaissance." Letter of 27 November 1850 from le Directeur général to le Ministre. Quoted in Courajod, *Histoire*, 201.

[24] "... un judieux esprit de classification scientifique." Courajod, *Histoire*, 239.

[25] The pieces already there by the 1850's included the tomb of Philippe de Commines and a thirteenth-century statue of King of Juda (Childebert) from S. Germain-des-Près.

[26] André Michel et Gaston Migeon, *Le Musée du Louvre: sculptures et objets d'art du Moyen Age, de la Renaissance, et des temps modernes* (Paris: Librarie Renouard. Henri Laurens, 1912).

27 On the Musée des Monuments Francais see Haskell. For a brilliant analysis of the Musee de Cluny, see Stephan Bann, "The Poetics of the Museum: Lenoir and du Sommerard," in *The Clothing of Clio: A Study in the Representation of History in Nineteenth Century Britain and France* (Cambridge UP, 1984). For an analysis of medieval museums in late nineteenth century France see Elizabeth Emery and Laura Morowitz, *Consuming the Past: The Medieval Revival in Fin de Siecle France* (London: Ashgate, forthcoming 2003), chapter 3.

28 Tony Bennet, *The Birth of the Museum: History Theory Politics* (London and New York: Routledge, 1995); Susan Pearce, ed. *Museums and Appropriation of Culture* (London: Athlone, 1994).

29 Paul Vitry, *The Museum of the Louvre: A Concise Guide to the Various Collections*, trans. Charles H. Hauff (New York: Gaston Braun, 1912).

30 Works from the seventeenth century and after were placed on the other side of the court, along the side of the Pont du Carousel and Rue de Rivoli.

A Birth Certificate for Sweden, Packaged for Postmodern: Jan Guillou's Templar Trilogy

Sandra Ballif Straubhaar

If you had asked a Swede five years ago to imagine a prototypical early ancestor for the Swedish nation – a Father of the Country, if you will – you would have been met first with utter bafflement, and then perhaps one of three answers: a Viking of Old Uppsala, quaffing mead out of a horn; Gustav Vasa, who led the Swedes to throw off Danish rule in 1520; or Birger Jarl, whom folklore credits with the founding of Stockholm in the thirteenth century. Had you even so much as suggested that the popular answer would soon be "A Knight Templar, of the Third Crusade," you would have been laughed at. But pan-Europeanism, as contrasted with Swedish uniqueness, is a force to be reckoned with in the new Sweden of the twenty-first century; as today's case study shows.

Similarly, if you had asked what authors and sources to turn to, for an inspiring Swedish national image of this kind, your informant would *not* have said, "a politically engaged print journalist of Franco-Norwegian ancestry, also known for popular spy novels, a painful autobiography, and 'how to hunt wild game' videos."

In five years, many things can change.

In any case, I present to you below four historical novels by a prominent Swedish writer and volatile public figure, who has most recently upset his fellow Swedes by his commentaries on connections between neopaganism and the skinhead movement, on Crown Princess Victoria's choice of dating partners, and on the potential role of social construction in same-sex attraction, as well as by walking out on the three minutes of silence at the Göteborg book fair in September 2001. He has also stirred unprecedented numbers of his fellow Swedes to go on pilgrimages, in the past five years or so, to the previously unvisited backwaters of Västergötland in western Sweden, in search of the (hypothetical) twelfth-century cradle of the Swedish nation…whereon hangs this article.

I will map out below how Jan Guillou was at first motivated to take a rhetorical swipe, through fiction, at Swedish xenophobia – specifically fears of immigrants from Islamic countries, which postmodern Sweden, like many other European nations of today, has many of. He found himself – almost coincidentally – participating in a broader project, crafting for role-model-hungry Swedes their own fictional ancestral prototype, in the form of returned crusader Arn Magnusson, and thus deliberately re-narrating his own nation's past, tweaking it toward the multicultural. Arn Magnusson is clearly a constructed figure – onomastics scholars could argue that even his name is a borrowed invention, and unattestable – but one who, in Guillou's own reassessment following the success of his novels, *ought* to have existed in real time. Guillou has actually commented recently that "Arn Magnusson fanns alltså. Han är vår landsfader" [So there really was an Arn Magnusson after all. He was the father of our country],[1] throwing light on his own views of that permeable boundary between verifiable history and legend-making in the fabrication of heroes and role models. We can see a Western-hemisphere parallel in the fact that it has not particularly mattered to north Americans that the historical Davy Crockett was, in fact, born on a mountaintop in North Carolina; what matters is that the Disney-generated figure of the plain-spoken, coonskin-capped frontiersman, incarnated in the person of Texan actor Fess Parker, became a role model for an entire generation – just as Guillou would like to see happen in today's Sweden with Arn Magnusson, his entirely fictional but typologically more or less accurate, multiculturally-enlightened Knight Templar.

Guillou's books about Arn and his kinfolk include:

(1) the trilogy of novels relating Arn's own life story, translated into many European languages and currently and/or about to be available in English from Orion Books, London:

Jan Guillou, *The Road to Jerusalem*. Trans. Anna Patterson (London: Orion, 2002).

Jan Guillou, *The Knight Templar*. Trans. Anna Patterson (London: Orion, 2002).

Jan Guillou, *Kingdom at the End of the Road*. Trans. Anna Patterson (London: Orion, 2003).

(2) a free-standing sequel about Birger Jarl, the historical founder of Stockholm and Arn's grandson in Guillou's fictional frame:

Jan Guillou, *Arvet efter Arn [Arn's Legacy]* (Stockholm: Piratförlaget, 2002); and

(3) a coffee-table photo book for tourists and pilgrims, including numerous photos, original art from two illustrators, and corroborative commentary from Dick Harrison, professor of history at the University of Lund:

Jan Guillou, et al, *I Arns fotspår [In Arn's Footsteps]* (Stockholm: Piratförlaget, 2002).

Since I have been following an ongoing Swedish neo-medieval revival movement for almost twenty years now, as an outside observer, I was naturally curious, when Jan Guillou's Arn books first began to come out, as to whether Guillou himself had any connection with the pan-Scandinavian roots-music phenomenon, for instance, currently occupied with reviving the medieval ballad tradition, among other things; or, perhaps more likely, with Swedish historical re-enactment events and pageants such as Hova riddarvecka (which revisits the year 1275; held every July since the 1980's) or Medeltidsveckan påGotland (which revisits the year 1361; held every August since 1983).[2]

It turned out, in any case, that Jan Guillou had had no connections with any such events or movements. In fact, as he told the Norwegian newspaper *Dagbladet* two years ago, he had, prior to the time of that interview, on several occasions been invited to speak at medieval-themed pageant events and been embarrassed to find himself the only participant dressed in a T-shirt and sport coat.[3] Now, of course, he knows better:

[Illustration: JG iförd sin Folkungamantel<http://members.tripod.com/manskara/images/n29.JPG>].

We will revisit the heraldry shown here later; but for now, take note of this fine blue velvet nobleman's cloak – clasped, although we can't see it from this angle, with a museum-reproduction high-medieval brooch – bought in Oslo, to the delight of Guillou's Norwegian fan base.[4]

I did find that Jan Guillou had been an avid reader of historical novels as a child; specifically, that he had read *Ivanhoe*, that is, Scott's original novel (independent of its film versions), with a flashlight under the bedclothes,[5] as any reader of *The Knight Templar* might suspect – since Wilfred of Ivanhoe himself appears in a walk-on cameo role toward the end of Guillou's book. I began also to suspect a childhood attachment to another well-known piece of medievalist fiction, namely, Harold Foster's *Prince Valiant*, from which Arn's name may well have been borrowed.

But the pre-Arn Magnusson Jan Guillou shows no other notable signs, as far as I can tell, of having been a life-long devotee of medieval history, or even of historical fiction, over and above his other admittedly wide-ranging interests. His heretofore best-known fictional protagonist, for instance, intelligence officer Count Carl Gustav Hamilton (code name Coq Rouge), came into being almost accidentally, following a long prison stay in which the writer devoured all the Martin Beck thrillers in the prison library and concluded that he could not only duplicate that genre, but improve upon it. As it turned out, I found, Arn Magnusson was also originally conceived in a similar cataclysmic moment.

Arn Magnusson, Guillou informs us, was "born" in a hotel room in Alma-Ata, Kazakhstan, in 1996, following forty-eight straight hours of watching CNN on cable while waiting for a phone call. (CNN was the only things available on TV in a language he understood). "It is a considerable mental ordeal for a print journalist," writes Jan Guillou, "to keep watching CNN for that long. You start having these dark doubts about the validity of your own work; about TV as a competent vehicle for news; or even about the free market as a competent vehicle for the truth."[6] By the time the phone finally rang, Guillou had checked off on scrap paper fifty-seven appearances on CNN of Muslims as "Bad Guys" and zero appearances of Muslims as "Good Guys," and, in addition, he had the bones of a fictional narrative already plotted out. Since not dissimilar holy wars, and not dissimilar demonization of one's enemy, could also be found in the historical past, he reasoned, a writer with a message to deliver could retell a story set in that historical past, allowing today to inform yesterday, if you will, with an eye toward reforming the attitudes of tomorrow.

The original plan, as Guillou mapped it out, was for a three-part story featuring a European who goes to the Crusades and afterward comes home, thereupon making home a different, and better, place. A Frenchman would be statistically most logical; but Guillou's first audience is Nordic, and so he made his hero a Swede – an option that would have been just barely possible in real history as we know it. (There is a Norwegian sidekick for part of the story. The Danes, alas, mostly get to be Bad Guys. But modern Danes seem to like the novels anyway). Obvious high points for narrative focus would be either the gain or the loss of Jerusalem; but the first of these would have been too brutal for Guillou's Crusader (as he anticipated his character to be like) to participate approvingly, while the second would carry more drama and sympathy for the losers. Thus the time-frame was established: our hero would be born about 1150, and come home some decades later.[7]

Here, with the grounding of the narrative in time, came the surprise bonus, previously unsuspected by the author, but soon discovered after research:[8] these decades are the very decades in which the kingdom of Sweden came to be. And so the foreign knowledge ([from a Cistercian monastery boyhood, in Denmark and Sweden] and from the Arab world) that Arn Magnusson (or Arn de Gothia, the Knight Templar) brings home to Sweden will turn out to be crucial in the formation of Sweden's very identity. Bingo! Grist for the rhetorical mill.

Now that the narrative foundations were set, Jan Guillou carefully selected two additional bricks for inclusion in the edifice. He had an auxiliary agenda from early on in the project, namely, to reappropriate Sweden's origins from the pagan Vikings of Old Uppsala, which every schoolchild knew about. He wanted to wrest the national origin-narrative away from a specific subset of those Vikings' modern admirers, namely, the Thor's-hammer-wearing promoters of Swedish Radical Purity who comprise a small, but loud, subgroup of Sweden's Generation X today.[9] In Arn Magnusson's Sweden, as Guillou foresaw it before writing, Christianity and a Christian world-view would be the seed-bed and the catalyst for progress and the future; there would be little nostalgia for lost pagan Viking ways. Thus Arn Magnusson – in ironic contrast to today's strikingly secular Swedes (as well as to his own, unbelieving author, for that matter)[10] – would begin and end the story as an unwavering Christian, just as convinced of the truths of his own belief system "as an editorial columnist for *Dagens Nyheter* in our own time," Guillou quips, notably implicating a rival newspaper, not his own.[11] Secondly, Arn Magnusson would come from western Sweden, from Västra Götaland – from the Götar, not the Svear – specifically *not* from the eastern homeland of those pagan Uppsala Vikings, some of whose descendants may well have still been pagan by Arn's era.

This choice of Götar (western clans) over Svear (eastern clans) as the chief founders of Sweden is hardly a closed case among Swedish historians, and has been the subject of fierce debate within academic memory; but it was now a necessary component of the narrative as planned, and so it had to go in. Guillou refers us, in the *Fotspår* volume, to researchers Dag Stålsjö, Michael Nordberg and Maja Hagerman as promoters of this version.[12] Like Japan's Hayao Miyazaki, who has similarly invoked historian Yoshihiko Amino's radical revision of his own nation's early past in his films, Jan Guillou is not above milking his own status as pop icon to promote his own didactic and propagandistic agendas by means of revised narrated pasts. Miyazaki has, in this paradigm, portrayed a more Koreanized early Japan, with more respect given to manual laborers than has been previously acceptable to the Japanese; Guillou has, in like fashion, portrayed a more multicultural early Sweden, coincidentally with more respect given to manual laborers, than has been previously acceptable to the Swedes. There is also much in common between Guillou's anti-xenophobic consciousness-raising project here and that of Norwegian anthropologist Thomas Hylland Eriksen, of the University of Oslo, who has delighted in pointing out to modern Norwegians (whom he sees as too provincial and isolationist for their own good) that many of the revered objects of unadulterated, ancient Norwegian-ness (such as the cheese cutter, the Hardanger fiddle, and the various national costumes) are neither particularly old, nor exclusively Norwegian.[13]

The appendix of quotations at the end of this article shows how Guillou's didactic agenda, on these and other fronts, manifests itself in the text. As the reader can observe, Guillou has taken pains, throughout the trilogy and its sequel, to present early Swedish progressive thinking (Arnian thinking, if you will) as marked by multiculturalism (quotations #3, 6, 7, 9, 11); egalitarianism, between social classes and the two genders (quotations #1, 4, 9, 10); pragmatism (quotations #2, 5, 6, 8, 12); and, precociously enough, separation between church and state, which Arn's grandson Birger Jarl is narrated as favoring (quotations #13 and 14).

One nonverbal strategy that Guillou has used to great advantage is that he has enlisted known heraldic symbols, already endowed with some emotional weight, to add verisimilitude and respectability to his story. Note the following:

[Illustration: Sveriges riksvapen: < http://www.svearike.com/riksvapen. htm>].

Within Guillou's narrative, the three-crown device becomes the personal arms of St. Erik, king of Sweden, and the father of Arn's best boyhood friend, Knut Eriksson, also king of Sweden; while the lion device becomes the ancient arms of the Folkung clan, which is Arn's own family. However, as the unofficial Swedish heraldry web site points out, neither of these devices is likely to be anywhere near as old as Arn is – although the traditional attributions are in fact as Guillou states.[14] Remember also that Jan Guillou – now that the popularity of his books, and their internal constructed history, has become assured – is now styling himself a member of the Folkung clan (see above) – though hardly as Arn the Templar. No, Guillou's twelfth-century Folkung self is also unmistakably his contemporary self, as we can see. He wears his Folkung arms with a postmodern difference: a little red writer's quill, signifying both his profession, and his politics.

Right now, if you're like me at all, you're probably asking yourself: how accurate is this narrated Middle Ages, presented to us by an author whose exposure to the Middle Ages before the project seems to have been exclusively on a popular-culture level? Are there any glaring anachronisms of the kind we love to spot? The short answer is ... no, not really – especially compared with the multitude of other popular narratives using pre-modern settings. Guillou claims to have read "meters' worth of bookshelves"[15] before beginning to write, and it shows.

One example may suffice. There is a great feast at Arn's father's homestead in the first chapters. A foreign skald is in attendance to recount the exploits of the Norwegian king Sigurd Jerusalem-farer; he accordingly recites some stanzas. I found the originals in E.A. Kock's *Skaldediktning*: Haldórr skvaldri, twelfth century.[16]

Since there are numerous times in the Arn Magnusson books when a reader might wonder what is invented and what is real, one can only concede that Guillou's art in blending the two is admirable. Guillou has obviously read his St. Bernard, and the Templar Rule; but one wonders if the Templars were *really* forbidden to launder their underwear. (Arn has to stand, and sit, downwind of his Saracen acquaintances because of this). Similarly, Guillou has obviously researched early, and rural, wedding customs; but one wonders if the charming athletic bachelor rituals that he describes so amusingly on several occasions – involving, for instance, the cleaving of maximum numbers of rotten turnips with one's sword from horseback – have any basis in reality. But this is all by way of admitting that the story does suck the reader in.

Historian Dick Harrison's corroborative essay in the *Fotspår* volume – although we have to consider that Harrison is constrained to be polite and reverential, as an invited contributor should be, in a volume printed by a publishing house in which Jan Guillou is the principal stockholder – seems almost to regret that he has only one "correction" to make to the text: Forsvik, one of the cradles of Swedish industry in both the narrated and the real past, and Arn's post-Crusades home in the novels, would have in fact been full of non-Swedes in early modern times; but these foreigners would have been Germans and Lithuanians, not the Arabs and Armenians they are in the books.[17] Obviously a German and Lithuanian presence in Forsvik would not serve Guillou's purposes as effectively. It is hardly surprising that when message contradicts history, history loses.

My final question today is, have these novels had a measurable effect on the behavior of today's Swedes, and other northern Europeans, as their author has intended them to? I can answer it with "Yes" on at least one front, besides the one already mentioned, the tourist pilgrimages to Vöstergötland. Suddenly, over the past several years, Medieval Week in Gotland – anachronistically enough, since, as you might recall, it's supposed to be 1361 in Gotland, and the Templars have been essentially out of commission since 1314 – has been invaded by burgeoning encampments of crusading Templar Knights.

UNIVERSITY OF TEXAS AT AUSTIN

Appendix: Polemical/Didactic Passages in Guillou's "Riddarsaga"
(translations S. Straubhaar)
1. Class conflict *extra mures* (Father Henri to Arn) (I:227)
   "...Out there they don't judge people by their souls... They see a king or a thrall, a jarl or a freedman. They see a man or a woman who has highborn ancestors, or who doesn't have them. Rather as you yourself and Brother Guilbert judge horses. That's how it is, out there in that other world."
2. Fear and Faith (Saladin and Arn) (II:31)
   "You are right, Templar," said Yussaf. "But tell me then: where is the dividing line between reason and faith, between fear and trust in God? If a man must obey as your sergeant must, does that diminish his fear?"
   "When I was young – not that I'm especially old now," said the Templar, "I thought about that kind of thing all the time. It's good exercise; working with the intellect flexes your thoughts. I'm afraid I'm out of practice now, though. One obeys. One defeats evil. One thanks God afterward. That is all there is to it."

"But if one doesn't defeat one's enemy?" asked Yussaf mildly...

"Then one dies. At least if one is Armand, or me," answered the Templar...

3. The Enemy is Just Like Us (Arn and Armand; city wall, Gaza) (II:139)

"First Saladin will show us his forces. And when he's done that, he'll show us his weapons – without meaning it seriously, though," answered Arn. It will be quiet in the first day, and only one man will die."

"Who will die?" asked Armand, wrinkling his forehead in puzzlement.

"A man your own age. A man like you," answered Arn almost mournfully. "A brave young man who believes that this is his chance to win great honor, and perhaps for the first time be part of a great victory. A man who believes that God is with him, despite the fact that God has already picked him out as the one who will die today."

Armand could not bring himself to ask more about the one who was going to die. His lord Arn had answered him as if he were far away in his thoughts, and as if his words perhaps meant something quite different than they seemed to mean on first hearing. The high brethren often spoke like that.

4. These Barbarians Can't Do Math; Cerebral Labor is Not Gender-Specific (Jöns, Cecilia Rosa, Mother Rikissa; Gudhem convent) (II:194 and 197)

Jöns the *yconomus* didn't even know how much money they had. He said he generally counted it by fistfuls. If there were more than ten fistfuls, it would last a good long time without needing more; if there were less than five fistfuls, then you were getting low...

Mother Rikissa tried weakly to object – no one had ever heard of a woman working as a *yconomus*. After all, that was why a masculine word was used to describe the position in the first place.

Cecilia Rose answered without hesitating that women were actually better suited to do this kind of work, in a nunnery. It wasn't the kind of work that required you to life a horse at arm's length, or to mortar together big stone blocks, now was it? If there was a problem with the title, they could just change the word. To *yconoma*.

5. Peace in the Middle East (II:256-7)

...Arnoldo de Torroja was, according to what Count Raymond had said, one of the few highly-placed Templars who understood the most important thing – the *only* important thing – relative to a Christian future in Outremer. Namely, to make peace with Saladin. Jerusalem would have to be divided, regardless of how painful that would be, so that all pilgrims – including the Jews – would have equal access to the city's sacred places.

There was only one other alternative. War with Saladin until he won a definitive victory and took Jerusalem by force. The problem was that with the current royal court in Jerusalem, there was no hope for anything other than that. They were dilettantes and schemers, and that was all they were good for.

6. Reason and Faith Again (Arn and Maimonides; Damascus, 1187) (II:407-8, 409-10)

When the Jewish physician patiently explained to Arn how Jerusalem was sacred to the Jews, and how the prophets had said that the Jews would return to reestablish their kingdom and rebuild their temple, Arn gave a deep sigh of sorrow. Not at the fate of the Jews, as he hastily explained when he saw how his new friend had interpreted his reaction, but at Jerusalem's. Soon the city would fall into Muslim hands, if it had not already done so. After that the Christians would spend all their strength to win it back. If the Jews were to get involved as well, the battle for Jerusalem might last for the next thousand years or more.

…When it came out that Arn could read Arabic, Musa ibn May-nun gave him a book he had written himself, called *Guide for the Perplexed*. Once Arn had gotten somewhat into the book, it gave new content for their conversations, because what Musa ibn May-nun strove for most in his philosophy was finding a balanced relationship between reason and faith, between Aristotle's teachings and the pure truth of revelation – which many people assumed to be independent of reason. To blend these apparent opposites together into one unity, he thought, was the most important task of philosophy.

7. Multicultural Irony: Mastery of One's Own Fate (II:415)

Arn sat for a time with the quill in his hand, staring at the empty parchment before him, trying to visualize himself and the world clearly in this incomprehensibly strange moment. He had to write his own letter of dismissal, and he was doing it in the sultan's palace in Damascus, sitting crosslegged on soft cushions in front of a Syrian writing desk with a turban wound around his head.

Many times in past years he had tried to imagine what it would be like when he would no longer be a Knight Templar. But even in his wildest fantasies he had not imagined anything like this.

At length he pulled himself together and quickly and confidently wrote out the text he knew so well, for in his term as Jerusalem's Master he had written a good many letters of this king. He also added a condition that was not without precedent: That this knight, who now with great honor terminated his service in God's Holy Army, the Templar Order, was free to go back to his former life, and that there also, whenever he found it fitting, he retained the right to clothe himself in Templar attire, of the rank that he had held when he left the Order.

He read the text through, and it came to his mind that Gerard de Ridefort did not know Latin; whereupon he added a translation in French.

Since there was still space remaining on the parchment, he could not resist the petty diversion of writing out the text a third time, for the benefit of the semi-literate Grand Master – this time in Arabic.

8. Good Uses for a King's Money (Arn and Knut Eriksson) (III:109)

"Build a monastery. Grand gold and forests. Build a church. Buy holy relics from Rome for the archbishop's cathedral. Do any of those things, or in extremity do all of them, before you call for a crusade. If you send any of the Folkings or the Erik clan to the Holy Land they will all be slaughtered like cattle, and to no earthly use. Only sorrow will come of it."

"And you know that of a certainty?" asked the king. "Is not the courage of our hearts enough, or the strength of our faith, or the might of our swords?"

"No!" said Arn.

A despondent silence fell over the room.

9. Manual Labor Knows No Rank (Arn and Magnus Månesköld) (III:179-183)

It all spun round in Magnus Månesköld's head until his eye settled on the mortar-splashed warrior's hand that was stretched out towards him; his eyes moved up, almost in horror, to the man's scarred face. His friends sat their horses in silence, fully as amazed as he.

"When your father reaches out his hand to you, I think you ought to take it," said Arn, smiling broadly, and wiping the sweat from his brow once again…

"You're hardly ready to travel, my father," Magnus said sullenly. "Thrall's clothes and mortar in one's hair aren't fitting for a bridegroom's fest."

"That's my opinion as well," Arn replied, as if he had not noticed that he had just been corrected by his own son…

But less than an hour passed by before an entirely different Arn Magnusson cam in through the door…

His foreign mail-shirt shone like silver, and fitted his body as well as if it were tailored from cloth. On his feet he wore a kind of steel shoes that none of the four friends had seen before, and on his heels were spurs of gold. Over the ring-mail he wore a Folkung tunic, and at his side hung a long, narrow sword in a black sheath inscribed with a gold cross…

As they rode out of the courtyard he turned his horse so that it danced round on its hind legs, and he drew his long, shining sword and called out something in a foreign language back towards the estate. The many foreigners answered him with laughter and cheering.

"He who judges hastily, judges his own self," said Torgils earnestly to Magnus, who was now occupied with mounting his own horse to follow after Arn.

10. Chivalry for Proles (Sigge and Orm, Gure the foreman, Arn) (III:368-375)

…Warrior-training was only for Folkungs, not for freedmen with names like Sigge, Toke, Luke or Orm. If you had a name like that, you were for the workshops.

Sigge clenched his teeth and said nothing. He'd been given a promise by Lord Arn, and he intended to remind Lord Arn of it when he got the chance…

"But my lord, these lads aren't any kind of Folkung," objected Gure in amazement.

"Well do I know that," said Arn. "They're nothing but a freedman's sons. But we had an agreement, and we Folkungs always hold to our agreements."

11. Imported Ideas (AA 196)

Things from the Southern lands were more often good than bad. Birger had always known that, since he'd grown up at Forsvik where so many things were a blend between northern and southern, so that Forsvik had become an oasis of knowledge and labor in a harsh land. He wasn't entirely sure what an oasis was, but it was a word everybody used at Forsvik.

12. Technology Wins the Day: Birger Invents Icebreakers (Birger Jarl and his brother Elof; Visby) (AA 344)

"So now we're going to free Lubeck out of king Erik Plowpenny's blockade, and if we manage that, neither you nor I will end up with empty pockets."

"You've got an army with you?" Elof burst out.

"No, I haven't. I have ten seasick smiths from Forsvik and a hold full of iron and gold, and that's all," Birger answered him mysteriously.

13. Literacy Through Alternative Venues (Birger Jarl, William of Sabina) (AA 380)

"…And that's why, Your Eminence, that in our land you can find more battle-scarred warriors who can speak Latin as well as I do than you'll find bishops who can. Especially bishops, I might add. We've got some who can't even read or write in the vernacular."

"I have noted that absurdity," answered the Cardinal, with raised brows.

14. Proto-Modern Thinking (Birger Jarl and Sir Sigurd [>Sigge]) (AA 415)

"I'm not a saint like he was. I didn't inherit that," Birger said with a shrug. "And besides that, Arn Magnusson was wrong in one important aspect, because even he wasn't infallible. Surely you remember how he used to say that power stood on three equally strong legs?"

"Yes. Gold, the sword, and the cross," answered Sigurd. "If we Folkungs controlled all three of these, then peace would last forever, and the land would blossom. And now you're telling me that you no longer believe in those principles?"

"Yes, I do believe in them, but only partially," Birger answered him. "Because soon we're going to cut ourselves loose from the Church, and leave the power than belongs to the cross in the hands of the Church's men. We won't interfere in what they do; they won't be able to meddle in the temporal sphere. And that leaves us standing on only two legs – gold, and the sword. But there's an important third leg as well: the law."

NOTES

[1] *Vi bilägare* (Swedish auto and travel magazine), #13, 2001.

[2] Ironically enough, although both of these events have become associated, in Swedish popular culture, with high chivalric heroism – of the sort associated with the Anthony Andrews-Olivia Hussey film of *Ivanhoe*, which Swedes have been watching on TV every Christmas since the 1980's – neither was originally founded on a particularly heroic historical prototype, but instead, perhaps with deliberate irony, on a *non*-heroic event. Gotland in 1361 was *invaded* by the Danish king Valdemar Atterdag; Hova in 1275 was the site of the *disposition* of king Valdemar Birgersson of Sweden by his two brothers.

[3] Eva Bratholm, "Guillous historiske oppgjør," *Dagbladet*, December 9, 2000.

[4] Bratholm.

[5] Guillou, *Fotspår*, 34.

[6] Guillou, *Fotspår*, 15.

[7] Guillou, *Fotspår*, 16.

[8] Guillou, *Fotspår*, 31.

[9] Guillou, *Fotspår*, 33.

[10] Guillou, *Fotspår*, 19.

[11] Guillou, *Fotspår*, 18.

[12] Guillou, *Fotspår*, 19, 30.

[13] See the chapter, "Myten om det homogene Norge," in Hylland Eriksen's book *Typisk norsk* (Oslo: C. Huifeldts forlag, 1993), for instance.

[14] Elias Granqvists sida om heraldic i Sverige [Elias Granqvist's Page on Heraldry in Sweden]. Available: <http://www.goto.Glocalnet.net/elias/heraldic.htm>.

[15] Guillou, *Fotspår*, 22.

[16] Ernst Albin Kock, ed., *Den norsk-isländska skaldediktningen* (Lund: Gleerup, 1946), pp. 225-7 and continuation of the anecdote, in the novel, Arn and his friend Knut Eriksson (the future king of Sweden), about five years old, are hiding under a leather cloak just outside the mead-hall door listening to the exciting stuff. They are supposed to be in bed. Knut's father, known to subsequent generations as St. Erik, staggers out, leans against the doorpost and pees on them.

[17] Guillou, *Fotspår*, 128.

Wholly Ghosts: Genre, Postmodern Transubstantiations and Flannery O'Connor's "The Enduring Chill"

Susan Rochette-Crawley

It is a common misperception that postmodernism, as a term used to define a time and its temper, is chiefly marked by the jettisoning of the past in favor of a present characterized primarily by chaos, decentralization, and linguistic mayhem. While the term first came into being as a heuristic for describing the conditions of life and language as they were being reconfigured in the wake of the Second World War, postmodernism often has been dogged by the attempt to define itself from within the midst of the very inarticulateness it seeks to describe. As a kind of global "spring cleaning of the soul," postmodernism found itself face-to-face with everything that had been stored in the collective basement of the "big house" of history, and, one by one, postmodernists discovered that things were in shabby disarray, in need of sorting, refurbishing, or discarding altogether. Of all traditional fields of study, the genre study is perhaps the one which has been most often tagged for garbage removal. If not for the New Historicism that was gathering strength simultaneous with the rise of postmodernism, genre study might not have survived this vigorous and somewhat antiseptic tendency to purge the past.

Yet, as Ralph Cohen points out in his article "Do Postmodern Genres Exist?," "every text is a member of one or more genres," and the postmodern enterprise is not to seek to deny genre, nor to perceive it as an essentially taxonomic exercise, but rather to study the "constituents of a text and what kinds of effects these have or can have upon readers."[1] He points out that even attempts to deny or degrade the study of genre themselves fall into the genres of satire, parody, and literary theory.[2] As to whether postmodern genres exist, Cohen emphatically defends their existence, and insists that the attempt to deny them only creates new ones for genre theorists to discuss. Furthermore, the postmodernist struggle with what to do with genre is not as contemporary a problem as one may think. The struggle with genre, its place, its nature, and its identity, is a particularly medievalist concern. Debates as to the nature of the *chanson de geste, epic, roman,* and, especially, *fabliaux,* have been current in the literature over time.[3] In this way, perhaps no area of study is as rich in postmodernist medievalisms as the study of genre. And, if Lyotard is right, that

> We no longer have recourse to the grand narratives – we can resort
> neither to the dialectic of Spirit nor even to the emancipation of
> humanity as a validation for postmodern scientific discourse ... the

little narrative [petit recit] remains the quintessential form of
imaginative invention, most particularly in science,[4]
then perhaps no other genre is as "postmodernly medieval" as the short
story, a genre timelessly given over to reinvention perpetually escaping
permanent definitions. And, of the short story masters of the pre-
postmodernist age whose work not only prefigures the post-existentialist
and postmodernist, none is better suited for a study of the survival of
the medieval in the postmodern than Flannery O'Connor.

Deceptively conservative in both her religious practice and her adherence
to Aristotelian and Thomist principles of art, Flannery O'Connor, in her
understudied story, "The Enduring Chill," combines a highly textualized
inquiry into the nature of the sacramental, as well as sacrilegious, body as it is
constituted in character and form. The story effectively performs a
postmodern transubstantiation of its generic identity as it simultaneously
engages in particularizing the "accidents" of story's sacramental elements:
word, image and fantastic intervention.

The popularity that the short fictive genre has always enjoyed, in one
form or another, continued strongly into and throughout the twentieth
century. A number of those included in the postmodern canon – Joyce,
Beckett, and Stein, for example – experimented in short narrative forms, and
Joyce's use of "epiphany" in *Dubliners* is often cited as an identifying quality of
the short story even into the present time. Italo Calvino, firmly situated in the
postmodern canon, preferred to work in the short narrative form, citing its
alignment with the swiftness of wit as one of its chief generic advantages.[5]
The history of the short story reveals that its generic specificity has always
eluded strict and total definition. While some view this as evidence that there
is nothing intrinsic to the genre to distinguish it from any other fictive
narrative, others have found this lack of strict definition and the genre's
perpetual ability to reinvent itself to be definitive of the short story form. In
any case, its plasticity as a narrative form renders it especially appropriate for
a discussion of medievalism and postmodernism.

Likewise, Flannery O'Connor has not until recently been studied in
relation to postmodernism, in spite of the fact that her many god-haunted
and existentially afflicted characters clearly indicate that her work entertains
postmodern concerns. Because O'Connor's art was principally informed by
Aristotelian principles of art and Thomist theology, and because both
Aristotle and Aquinas are reflexively considered to be antithetical to anything
that might be called postmodern, O'Connor is most frequently read as an
American regionalist or as what can loosely be called a "Catholic writer." Yet
a postmodernist reading of Thomist theology itself, as it pertains especially to

the Eucharist, assists in understanding the postmodern nature of O'Connor's work, particularly in the story "The Enduring Chill."

Regarding the specific character of the Eucharist as a sacrament, Aquinas insists that the accidents, or materials, of the Eucharist must be wheat bread and wine, though he allows that it is not as important whether the bread be either leavened or unleavened, except according to either the Roman or Eastern rites, respectively.[6] In this much, Aquinas admits of and encourages respect for both tradition and diversity in the interest of the catholic identity of the church. Inasmuch as postmodernism acknowledges above all divergence, multiplicity, and equivalence, Aquinas, for all his conservatism, shares a nascent sense of the postmodern condition of plurality. But it is in his defense of the nature of the accidents of bread and wine, which remain after consecration, that Aquinas prefigures existentialist thought.

Aquinas addresses, in Question 77, Article 1 of *Summa Theologica*, the nature of the accidents of bread and wine upon consecration. Aquinas maintains that the accidents themselves, though still visible as bread and wine, no longer remain but literally become the body and blood of Christ. Aquinas' radical literalism in his understanding of the Eucharistic transformation is, post-Reformation, a major stumbling block to ecumenical communion between the Roman and Protestant churches. At the same time, it is through the reasoning whereby he explains how the accidents remain in the sacrament without being subject to their own substance that he articulates a medieval existentialism. According to Aquinas, though the bread and wine remain after consecration, yet they are not, having now become the literal body and blood of Christ, any longer subject to being, in substance, either bread and wine. For, according to Aquinas, "Since being is not a genus, then it cannot be of itself the essence of either substance or accident."[7] In other words, being is something other than corporeality and is not in itself either substance or accident. In the case of the Eucharist, the bread and wine are simply accidents, things designated by chance, and their subjectivity as body and blood of Christ, divinely bestowed, exists quite apart from the materials of the sacrament simultaneously as their visible presence as bread and wine remain. The Thomist defense of sacramentalism, then, is not at all unlike the existentialist position that Being is something in itself, apart from the "accidents" of the flesh, or even the corporeal subjectivity of the one who calls self "I." The deconstruction of the Cartesian subject is nothing if not a postmodernist enterprise. And, in Aquinas' explanation of the simultaneous presence of bread and wine as both devoid of and invested with subjectivity, resides what Bakhtin might call an "historical inversion" of the postmodern anxiety of existence within the medieval systematic.[8]

O'Connor came to the question of the nature of existence not as a theologian but through the menial task of attempting to fashion an art from her knowledge of the world in its material and spiritual dimensions. In this, her artistic aesthetic was formed by the French Thomist, Jacques Martain. In her speech, "The Nature and Aim of Fiction," O'Connor cites Martain's famous concept of the "habit of art," by which, according to O'Connor, "habit" in this sense means a certain quality or virtue of the mind. "The scientist has the habit of science; the artist, the habit of art."[9] In that same essay, O'Connor explains her aesthetic in simple terms. "The person who aims after art," says O'Connor, "aims after truth, in an imaginative sense, no more and no less. St. Thomas said that the artist is concerned with the good of that which is made; and that will have to be the basis of my few words on the subject of fiction."[10]

For O'Connor, as a practicing Catholic of the Roman rite, the sacrament of the Eucharist, as an "outward and visible sign of an inward and spiritual Grace," was the spiritual food that nourished her soul as believer and artist. The incarnation of the Eucharist and the carnal nature of art are not, for O'Connor, sundered or incompatible. Rather, art and divinity travel along parallel lines, intersecting through the movement of Grace, embodied in Christian iconography, principally as the Holy Ghost. O'Connor admits that as an artist of faith, nothing is more difficult than depicting the presence of supernatural Grace in fiction. "We almost have to approach it negatively," she says in a letter to Eileen Hall.[11] In "The Enduring Chill," O'Connor culminates the drama of Grace and ontology in Asbury's chilling knowledge that in fact he knows nothing. His existential condition will not change, yet he effectively ascends by means of his descent, and is terrifyingly Graced by his encounter, with the Holy Ghost descending upon him at the end of the story.

The "accidents" of the story that are associated with both the Holy Ghost and the communion wafer are sacramentalized in the first paragraph, as Asbury descends from the train to greet his mother. Her face is "thin," "spectacled" and "bright." Her smile "vanishes" "suddenly" upon seeing his ill condition, and, for Asbury, "The sky was a chill gray and a startling white-gold sun, like some strange potentate from the east, was rising beyond the black woods that surrounded Timberboro." He feels he is about to experience some "majestic transformation," and the roofs of the town look like "mounting turrets of some exotic temple for a god he didn't know."[12] The entire story rebounds with images of pale round shapes, eyes, spectacles, orbs, "rare coins," as well as "moments of communion" and instructions to "open your mouth."

If the one-to-one correspondence between images of the Holy Ghost and symbolic references to the Holy Host were the principle means that

O'Connor used to effect the meaning of the story, then early critics who misread her work as thinly veiled papist propaganda could have been correct in dismissing her as an artist. However, within the story, and, in fact through the very circularity of the short story form itself, O'Connor effects a postmodern turn, both in form and content.

Anthony Di Renzo has noted the "Felliniesque quality" of Asbury's deathbed imaging of his own funeral,[13] but little discussion is made of the curious conversation Asbury has with the priest, Father Finn, who ostensibly is brought in by his mother. While it appears that, in the material "accidents" of the story – the call for a priest, the summoning of one by Asbury's mother, and the entry of the priest into the room -- the reader is to take the priest's presence literally, the priest himself, a Grim Reaper figure "who plowed straight across the room" introduces himself in such a way as to provide the literal point in the story where fantastic intervention temporarily intercedes and raises the story itself to the level of postmodern self-reflexivity.

The story has been set up in such a way as to make the reader anticipate a dire, if not violent, ending. Yet, in the oral resonance in "Father Finn's" introduction the story – "'I'm Fahther Finn – from Purrgatory,'" he said in a hearty voice" – the reader is transported, by means of textual embedding, or generic ascension through descent, to internal questions not only of faith and salvation, but also of genre. Asbury, sure that now amidst his dreariness he has found an intelligent person to talk with regarding matters of art and existence, asks the priest – "I wonder what you think of Joyce, Father?" The priest, who is "Blind in one eye and deaf in one ear," needs the question repeated. "What do you think of Joyce?" Asbury said louder. "Joyce? Joyce who?" asked the priest. "James Joyce," Asbury said and laughed. The priest brushed his huge hand in the air as if he were bothered by gnats. "I haven't met him, he said."[14]

It is impossible not to know that O'Connor was having fun with her genre and its most renowned innovator, James Joyce. "Epiphany," as first employed by Joyce in *Dubliners*, a collection of stories that is loosely regarded as a short story cycle, had, by O'Connor's time, become a generic code word for the effect toward which a story is to aim. That O'Connor was a Roman Catholic short story writer who claims not to have even heard of, much less read, Joyce until she went to the Writer's Workshop in Iowa City seems nearly impossible to believe except that this is what she writes in one of her letters to "A," dated 28 August 1955.[15] In a letter, again to "A," dated 21 February 1957, while she was at the time working on the story "The Enduring Chill," O'Connor recommended that "A" buy *Dubliners* and read the stories "because," as O'Connor writes, "you can learn an awful lot from them."

That O'Connor struggled with her appreciation of and regard for Joyce is legendary. But it is also revealing that in her letter to Father John McCown, dated January 16, 1956, she mentions Joyce and the Holy Ghost in nearly the same breath: "you get more benefit reading someone like Hemingway, where there is apparently a hunger for a Catholic completeness in life, or Joyce who can't get rid of it no matter what he does. It may be," she writes, "a matter of recognizing the Holy Ghost in fiction by the way He chooses to conceal himself."[16] By embedding the "(w)holly ghost" of Joyce, her greatest predecessor in the genre for which she herself has become most famous, in the story "The Enduring Chill" O'Connor is not so much revealing an anxiety of influence as she is trying to "purge" her own storytelling of limits resulting from the generic constraints imposed by the valorizing of "epiphany" as both the end and the aim of the modern short story. Epiphany, as Joyce describes its artistic nature, was a "sudden manifestation" for either or both character and reader. Ostensibly the epiphany in a story would clinch for the reader, thus revealing the cleverness of the writer, a moment of aesthetic transcendence which, in Joyce's work, most often culminates in a disdain for the world. For O'Connor, who worked more on the precipice of the postmodern realization that "manifestations" or sudden outward signs invested with meaning are not the end in themselves, but rather turn one back in upon the possibility that Mystery endures, Asbury's "epiphanic" moment has meaning only if it turns him *away from* worldly manifestations and *towards* the inward stillness of contemplation. And, as any Thomist knows, contemplation is not a call to renounce the world but to fully engage with it in all its materiality.

The degree to which this is possible is evident in Asbury's final vision of the Holy Ghost, configured in a water stain on the ceiling, descending over him as he lies abed, sentenced not to death but to life, to his own "being in nothingness." Asbury's vision, or his epiphany, does not perform the same way that Gabriel's does in "The Dead." Gabriel too is sentenced to live with unbearable knowledge – the knowledge that in fact he has not lived at all – and in both stories the images of snow and ice fix or paralyze the respective characters. Yet there is an important difference, implicit in the openings of each story. In Joyce's story, the opening scene suggests a bustle of life and history out of which Gabriel progresses, through the convention of accumulating knowledge, *toward* the epiphany as a kind of "final awareness." In *Dubliners*, Joyce was still of the mind that while history could not be denied, it might be possible to transcend it aesthetically. In "The Enduring Chill," however, the end of the story necessarily sends the reader back to the beginnings of Asbury's history, rooted in the post-industrial, anti-intellectual climate of the fundamentalist American South. Thus, Asbury's epiphanic moment, which leads not to transcendence of the body but to a horrifyingly real possibility that there is no relief from corporeality, makes a full circle and arrives at a point of completion, albeit that completion suggests that without the Grace bestowed by the Holy Ghost, existence is little more than tautological. The only alternative to this existence, as O'Connor saw it, was to return to Mystery, in all its sacred sacrilegiousness. O'Connor, unlike Joyce, who saw the abyss and retreated from it into his art, welcomed, invited and courted the abyss, as an opportunity for renewal of faith. And, in fact, when asked once what a short story was, O'Connor answered in true postmodernist form by describing what it was *not*, except to say it must always lead toward death and mystery. This principle is enacted in her story by a peculiarly postmodern medieval systematic, an existential Thomism that is underscored by her love for her grotesque and beset characters. O'Connor effects a postmodern transubstantiation of her genre through the very physical, literal accidents of sacramental art, extending even the form, as well as the content, of the story. To a great extent, it can be said that O'Connor, in her persistent faith in what can be called "medieval knowledge," enacts in her "petit recit" the "thorough exteriorization of knowledge with respect to the 'knower,' at whatever point he or she may occupy in the knowledge process," which Lyotard claims postmodern individuals can come to expect.[17] And harkening back to the initial question regarding genre in the postmodern era, Lyotard himself answers the ontological question regarding postmodern genres when he says, "If there are no rules, there is no game."[18] It would be easy to imagine O'Connor answering, as she once did about the need for a story to have a beginning, middle and end: "Yes, but not necessarily in that order." After all, within the hermeneutic circle her stories trace, all roads lead to the same destination, and everything that rises must converge.

UNIVERSITY OF NORTHERN IOWA

NOTES

[1] Marjorie Perloff, *Postmodern Genres* (Norman: U of Oklahoma P, 1989), 14.

[2] Perloff, 20.

[3] Norris J. Levy, in his *Reading Fabliaux* (New York: Garland, 1993, p. 23), notes the debate in Paul Zumthor's *Essai de poetique medievale* (Paris: Seuil, 1972). Zumthor, it can be argued, is a postmodern medievalist of the earliest school of postmodernist thought, perhaps one of those postmodernists who were "armed and dangerous" with their brooms and scouring pads while rummaging through the "big house" of critical thought.

[4] Jean Francois Lyotard, *The Postmodern Condition* (Minneapolis: U of Minnesota P), 60.

[5] Italo Calvino, *Six Memos for the Next Millenium* (New York: Garland, 1993), 35.

[6] Thomas Aquinas, *Summa Theologica* (Vol. V IIIa QQ. 74-90). Fathers of the English Dominican Province (Westminster: MD, 1948), 2436.

[7] Thomas Aquinas, *Summa Theologica* (Vol. V IIIa QQ. 74-90), 2457.

[8] In his *Existentialism and Thomism* (New York: The Philosophical Library, Inc., 1960), Joseph C. Mihalich explains Aquinas' thought as an existential rather than essential metaphysic precisely along these lines. "Existence or the 'act of *to be*' is the focal point and frame of reference in this metaphysical approach. When we say 'an essence *is*' we strike at the heart of reality – we sublimate the notion the notion of essence in stressing the existential factor or act of existing. Existence or the act of *to be* in itself is not a thing or a nature of essence. Thus we know *existence* itself or the act of *to be* by a different function of the mind than we know an essence or a nature" (73). I would contend that it is by means of her art that O'Connor articulates the 'different function of mind' whereby nature and essence are known.

[9] Flannery O'Connor, *Mystery and Manners* (New York: Noonday, 1961), 64-5.

[10] Flannery O'Connor, *Mystery and Manners*, 65.

[11] *The Habit of Being: Letters of Flannery O'Connor*, ed. Sally Fitzgerald (New York: Farrar, Straus, Giroux, 1979), 144.

[12] Flannery O'Connor. *Everything That Rises Must Converge* (New York: Farrar, Straus and Girroux, 1993), 82). In a letter to her then anonymous friend, "A," O'Connor explained that Allen Tate, upon reading an early version of the story, advised her to "get the Holy Ghost in the first page or two. That is very good advice and that is what I have proceeded to do." Fitzgerald, 261.

[13] O'Connor, *Everything That Rises Must Converge*, 105.

[14] Flannery O'Connor. *Everything That Rises Must Converge* (New York: Farrar, Straus and Girroux, 1993), 105.

[15] Fitzgerald, 97.

[16] Fitzgerald, 130. The degree to which O'Connor's conversational remark prefigures the entire Derridean precept of presence being marked by absence cannot be overlooked.

[17] Lyotard, 4.

[18] Lyotard, 10.

"The Accuracies of My Impressions": Mark Twain, Ford Madox Ford, and Michael Crichton Re-Imagine Chivalry

David Lampe

"The more ignorant men are, the more convinced are they that their little parish and their little chapel is an apex to which civilization and philosophy has painfully struggled up the pyramid of time from a desert of savagery."[1]

All fiction is historic, set, after all, in imaginary times which, as soon as the novel is finished, becomes the past. Yet as William Gass observes, "To call a novel historical is nearly always to accuse it of something."[2] So better than making and accusations or disclaimers, let me instead suggest that "historical fiction"[3] tells us as much about the awareness and values of the author and his age as it does about the past it presents. This is especially true of the three time-travel novels addressed in this essay: Mark Twain's *Connecticut Yankee in King Arthur's Court* (1889), Ford Madox Ford's *Ladies Whose Bright Eyes* (1911, 35), and Michael Crichton's *Timeline* (1999); a late nineteenth-century satire, a high modernist response, and the speculative effort of a popular postmodern writer. Of these three, Mark Twain's *A Connecticut Yankee* is the best known, though I will argue that Ford's *Ladies Whose Bright Eyes* deserves equal attention and even more praise.

I.

All three novels explicitly juxtapose the past and present. "It was in Warwick Castle," Twain announces, "that I came across the curious stranger," Hank Morgan, the practical Yankee who will be his narrator and protagonist. After meeting Hank, Twain spends a rainy night:

> from time to time I dipped into old Sir Thomas Malory's enchanting book, and fed at its rich feast of prodigies and adventures, *breathed in the fragrance of its obsolete names*, and dreamed again.[4]

And certainly Malory provides both the world of dream and stylistic fragrance for Twain, as well as Hank, who describes himself as "a Yankee of the Yankees – and practical; yes, and nearly barren of sentiment, I suppose – or poetry, in other words."[5] Twain describes Hank's "journal," his source, as a palimpsest. Twain tell us it is made up of "Latin words and sentences; fragments from old monkish legends."[6] Yet as close as Twain really comes to a medieval source is Malory, his and Hank's real source. Indeed, *CY* might itself be described as a Malory palimpsest. Twain actually treats Malory as a quaint, and perhaps less clumsy, James Fenimore Cooper. After this first episode, Twain uses five other Malory episodes, which he alternately reinscribes and ridicules.

Twain is efficient in managing Hank's time travel. The plot trigger is a fight in the Colt foundry, "a misunderstanding conducted with crowbars with a fellow we used to call Hercules. He laid me out with a crusher alongside the head that made everything crack."[7] When he comes to, his is "sitting under an oak tree, on the grass, with a whole beautiful and broad country landscape all to myself except for a horseman 'fresh out of a picture book'":

> He was in old-time iron armor from head to heel, with a helmet on his head the shape of a nail-keg with slits in it; and he had a shield, and a sword, and a prodigious spear; and his horse had armour on, too, and a steel horn projecting from his forehead, and gorgeous red and green silk trappings that hung all around him like a bed-quilt, nearly to the ground.[8]

Always a utilitarian, Hank describes the helmet, shield, sword, and spear before the silk, and assumes his subject must be from a circus. But when they do not come to any circus" he decides he must be "from an asylum."[9] Only later does Hank learn that it is "528 – nineteenth of June"[10] or as he puts it "A.D. 528, O.S."[11] At King Arthur's court he notices that along with being "gracious and courtly," they are quite credulous:

> They were a childlike and innocent lot; telling lies of the stateliest pattern with a gentle and winning naiveté, and ready and willing to listen to anybody else's lie, and believe it, too.[12]

The stoicism of prisoners around the Round Table makes Hank realize that

> They were not expecting any better treatment than this; so their philosophical bearing is not an outcome of mental training, intellectual fortitude, reasoning; it is mere animal training; they are *white Indians*.[13]

This credulity he finds "very engaging" and with typical Twainian oversimplification asserts that "boys are the same in all ages."[14]

Yet Hank goes out of his way to burlesque Malory lest it affect this "young adult audience." Certainly part of Hank's discontent comes from his attitude toward nobility; Citizen Hank Morgan is on the side of the "ever memorable and blessed [French] Revolution."[15] Yet he repeats the same excesses as that age. After he saves himself by anticipating an eclipse, Hank establishes himself as "The Boss" and concludes that "What this folk needed, then, was a Reign of Terror and a guillotine."[16]

What I am suggesting then is that we have an unreliable narrator. A clear suggestion of this is Hank's aesthetic. His vision of art is the chromo, those gaudy Victorian color pictures made of aluminum and zinc which, like everything else in Hank's world, is valued for its realism:

> We had several of [Raphael's] chromos; one was his "Miraculous
> Drought of Fishes," where he puts in a miracle of his own — puts
> three men into a canoe which wouldn't have held a dog without
> upsetting. I always admired to study R's art, it was so fresh and
> unconventional.[17]

In chapter nine, Hank comments on the reporting of tournaments.[18] Hank
finds "its antique wording was quaint and sweet and simple."[19] But it is also a
transparent lie. "There was never such a country for wandering liars; and they
were of both sexes:"

> Hardly a month went by without one of these tramps arriving: and
> generally loaded with a tale about some princess or other wanting
> help to get her out of some far-away castle where she was held in
> captivity by a lawless scoundrel, usually a giant. Now you would think
> that the first thing the king would do after listening to such a
> novelette from an entire stranger, would be to ask for credentials —
> yes, and a pointer or two as to locality of castle, best route to it, and
> so on. But nobody ever thought of so simple and common-sense a
> thing as that. No, everybody swallowed these people's lies whole, and
> never asked a question of any sort or about anything.[20]

When Hank is given the opportunity of experiencing one of these adventures
he is "as glad as a person is when he is scalped,"[21] and begins questioning
Demoiselle Alisandre la Carteloise regarding "particulars:"

> 'Where do you live when you are at home? Your name, please?
> …Have you brought any letters — any documents — any proofs that
> you are trustworthy and truthful?'[22]

He is especially frustrated when she doesn't even know what a map is. Yet as
they travel, Hank cannot resist searching for these essential narrative *facts*:

> The truth is. Alisande, the archais are a little too simple; the
> vocabulary is too limited, and so by consequence, descriptions suffer
> in the matter of variety; they run too much to level Saharas of fact,
> and not enough to picturesque detail; this throws about them a
> certain air of the monotonous; the fights are all alike.[23]

Even worse regional dialect, that true mark of local color, is violated:

> Sir Marhaus the king's son of Ireland talks like all the rest; you ought
> to give him a brogue, or at least a characteristic expletive; by this
> means one would recognize him as soon as he spoke; without his
> ever being named. It is a common literary device with the great
> authors. You should make him say 'In this country, be jabbers, came
> never knight since it was christened, but he found strange adventures,
> be jabbers.' You see how much better that sounds.[24]

Hank is practicing the same kind of nitpicking criticism that Twain himself exercised on Fenimore Cooper. He finally concludes

> Knights errant were not persons to be believed – that is measured by modern standards of veracity; yet measured by the standards of their own time, and scaled accordingly, you got the truth. It was very simple; you discounted a statement 97%; the rest was fact.[25]

But this might also describe Twain's own procedure. Instead of having Indians who miss the canoe, he reduces his knights to traveling salesmen "bearing one device or another" to sell soap or stove polish while riding bicycles rather than horses. Hank explains "It was another of my surreptitious schemes for extinguishing knighthood by making it grotesque and absurd."[26]

Yet amidst all of this, Hank is not without his own illusions. His anti-clericalism blinds him, and his rivalry with Merlin leads to the dark apocalyptic end of the novel, which seems to anticipate the horrors of trench warfare:

> I touched a button, and shook the bones of England loose from her spine!
> In that explosion all our noble civilization-factories went up in the air and disappeared from the earth. It was a pity, but it was necessary. We could not afford to let the enemy turn our own weapons against us.[27]

And so instead of improving the world of the past, Hank destroys all order:

> We are done with the nation; henceforth we deal only with the knights. English knights can be killed, but they cannot be conquered. We know what is before us. While one of these men remains alive, our task is not finished, the war is not ended. We will kill them all.[28]

II.

Ford Madox Ford's *Ladies Whose Bright Eyes* is quite a different matter. It first appeared in 1911, was reprinted in 1919 and 1931, and was seriously revised in 1935. Like Twain, this novel wastes little time returning its protagonist to the medieval past, though in this case it is to the fourteenth century rather than Twain's quasi-Arthurian sixth century. The novel's title comes from Milton's "L'Allegro:"

> Towered cities please us then
> And the busy haunts of men
> Where throngs of knights and barons bold
> In weeds of peace high triumphs hold,
> With store of *ladies whose bright eyes*
> Rain influence and judge the prize.[29]

It is these "bright eyes," the female gaze, that establishes and controls the actions of the novel. What Ford calls "the two stranded idea" of the novel establishes connections between the ladies of the present and past. The nun on the train "had very red cheeks, as if she had been much in the open air, blue rather hard eyes" and "large teeth."[30] In the fourteenth-century world he sees a nun who "had red cheeks, large teeth, and a kind smile."[31] She speaks "Some South French dialect" and her eyes "were large and eager."[32] Sorrell "champions"[33] Mrs. Lee-Egerton who is "very dark and very tall and very aquiline" and "exceedingly thin."[34] She has "enormous tears in her enormous eyes."[35] When she worries that her son Jack "might have to go to prison she shuddered all over her long and snake-like body."[36] Sorrell, "rising forty" and "typical Homo Sapiens Europaeus,"[37] responds by lending her money, and he is given "the Tamworth-Egerton crucifix" as security. Yet when Sorrell looks at it he wonders about its "inestimable value:"[38]

> Mr. Sorrell opened the leather case and looked at the battered, tarnished, light gold object. It was about the size of a dog biscuit and the thickness of a silver teaspoon. The cross was marked upon the flat surface with punched holes much like those on the surface of a dog biscuit itself.[39]

When a track accident sends him back to the fourteenth century, this cross is fiercely disputed by Lady Blanche de Coucy d'Enguerrand and Lady Dionissia de Egerton de Tamworth. Lady Blanche has "hot green eyes"[40] that smolder with fire[41] and are "alight with the contagion of enthusiasm,"[42] like her kisses. Three times she swears "By the eyes of Christ."[43]

Lady Dionissia is nineteen, "tall, large-limbed," and, unlike dark Blanche, "of an exceeding and most unusual fairness."[44] She turns "her deep and bewildered glances upon Mr. Sorrell," who comes to be aware of this "fixed and bemused glance."[45] "Her blue eyes" command "him beneath their dark brown brows"[46] and she tells Sorrell "When I first set eyes upon you I knew that I loved you."[47] She has "extreme physical strength,"[48] and when at the end of the novel she kills the Young Knight to revenge his wounding of Sorrell, "Her eyes were enormously large and stared hardly, like two blue stones."[49]

Even the less important ladies are characterized by their eyes. Sister Radigunda's "eyes shone with a dark fury"[50] while the almoner "rolled large eyes of appeal;" and the Abbess "blinked her eyes."[51] The Queen "was a fat matron," whose "eyes were small, brown, and keen."[52]

The Egerton-Tamworth cross is another link between the past and present. Sorrell enacts the role of the legendary Greek slave bringing it back to England. It is also credited with two miracles: the cure of a beggar and rescue from bandits. But we readers know that both of these are falsely ascribed, especially the latter which is achieved by "an immense white horse."[53] Yet Ford is not as dismissive of fourteenth-century values as Twain, though initially Ford's Sorrell is quite contemptuous of the world he enters. Like Hank, he believes in modern technology:

> What a bully time he might have had if with all his present faculties and knowledge he could be thrown right back into the Middle Ages – when the world had been full of nuns. What would not he be able to do with those ignorant and superstitious people.[54]

Like Hank, Sorrell is transported back to an earlier time by an accident, in his case a train wreck rather than a crowbar. Although he recognizes "Salisbury Spire," he is distressed by "carcasses that were dangling from the oak tree."[55] It must, he decides, all be part of a "pageant" since "there were pageants in every corner of England."[56] A confirmed modern skeptic, he suspects that the castle he sees "probably contained automobiles."[57]

> Mr. Sorrell let himself drop into the role of the dispassionate spectator. No one appeared to notice his garments. The pageant itself was really interesting. It might almost have been real life.[58]

Yet this condescending detachment doesn't last for long. He is an excellent linguist and when his use of modern French idiom fails, he comes to a recognition:

> And, with a queer start, he found that he was not any longer thinking of these people as taking part in a pageant. They must, if they were, have been playing it for at least twenty years. Their lances were old and rusty, handling, their clothes very worn ... He could not get away from the feeling that they were living their normal lives.[59]

Indeed, he will accept the virtues and values of this age over his own. Central to this process is a recognition of difference, especially in language. Unlike Hank, who tries to reform narrative according to the practices of nineteenth-century journalism, it is the people of the past who charitably make allowances for Sorrell's "odd perversion of French French."[60] In most ways, the language of the past is superior:

> He found that when he talked French very slowly and distinctly the little boy understood him. And the little boy had such a fluting grave voice that he himself had little difficulty in understanding his answers.[61]

The same change of attitudes takes place regarding social institutions. Even though (or is it because?) Sorrell is the publisher of popular encyclopedias (Ford corrected entries for the eleventh edition of the Britannica which appeared in the same year as the first version of the novel), Sorrell initially assumes that "Life in the Middle Ages was a simple affair. He did not suppose that they actually had any laws at all"[62] until he overhears "what they were carrying on now was rather more complicated than an average argument about mining rights in the Court of Chancery."[63] This level of sophisticated efficiency forces him to recognize unexpected social variety; "in other countries they have other customs,"[64] and the first section of the novel ends with Sorrell observing, "There doesn't seem to be any end to all this washing."[65] Hardly an expectation he would have had regarding the "Dark Ages."

The direction of Ford's novel then is the exact opposite of Twain's:

> 'I don't want to get back into my past,' Mr. Sorrell said. 'I wonder now that I could ever have lived it. It appears little and grey and cold and unimportant. I don't know what could have kept me going then.'[66]

Of course what keeps him going and changes his whole perspective is his love for Lady Dionissia. His need to master the world is gone. "'Now I don't care, I don't care for anything but walking in the fields and talking to you.'"[67] In an "Envoi," he returns to the present to be joined with the nurse who saved him, Dionissia Morane. In the 1911 novel, he aims to rebuild the "an exact reproduction of a fourteenth-century castle,"[68] only to have this passion "very sensibly diminished" by Girton-educated Morane, so instead the castle is turned into "an exceedingly comfortable dwelling-house":[69]

> Dionissia is convinced, that one century is as good as another. And just as bad. We aren't so adventurous as we used to be, but we don't go in for so many lawsuits. We aren't so romantically dressed, but we have got electric light and better baths … Romance, according to Dionissia, is the flavour of any life at any time. It's the reckoning up of success or failure at the end of things.[70]

III.

Our third novel, Michael Crichton's *Timeline*, is not as efficient, or perhaps as interested in, returning to the past. Instead, Crichton gives us a great deal of quasi-information about quantum mechanics. It takes one hundred and eighty pages to get back to fourteenth-century France. Yet despite a four-page, seventy-two item bibliography, and even an epilogue, Crichton really writes a modern gothic novel, a more specialized form of historical fiction. His characters are not based on historical or mythical prototypes (as in *Connecticut Yankee*) or given any real depth of characterization (as in *Ladies Whose Bright Eyes*). Instead, the novel is plot driven, and we read it wondering what will happen rather than why or to whom. What Crichton seems most interested in is a critique of modern scientific and capitalist consumer assumptions. Robert Doninger, a villain of the work is an insensitive genius turned to superconductive magnetism (MRI machines), and as a billionaire finally founds ITC (International Technology Corporation). He is wealthy enough to buy a Gutenberg Bible and Rouen Tapestry,[71] but seems most skilled as a spin-master touting the "promise of the past:"

> "Sooner or later," he said, "the artifice of entertainment – constant, ceaseless entertainment – will drive people to seek authenticity. *Authenticity* will be the buzz word of the 21 century. And what is authentic? Anything that is not controlled by corporations. Anything that is not devised and structured to make a profit. Anything that exists for its own sake, that assumes its own shape. And what is the most authentic of all? The past ...
>
> The past is a world that already existed before Disney and Murdock and British Telecom and Nissan and Sony and IBM and all the other shapers of the present. The past was here before they were ... The past is real. It's authentic. *And that will make the past unbelievably attractive.* Because the past is the only alternative to the corporate present.[72]

Having made his point that "history is the most powerful intellectual tool a society possesses," Doninger insists "the future lies in the past."[73] Yet at the end of novel his past turns on him, and his board replaces him with someone more moderate and transports him to the fourteenth century amidst the flagellants of the Black Death.

Despite his careful attention to most detail, Crichton is about as sensitive to fourteenth-century language as Twain was to that of the sixth century. While he recognizes French language differences (Occitan and Middle French) and even equips his time-travelers with machine translators and radio language microphones, his understanding of Middle English is Maloryese at its worst.

> Chris gradually fell to saying 'Methinks' instead of "I think" and "an" instead of "if" and "forsooth" instead of "in truth." And with each small change the boy seemed to understand him better.[74]

In fact, he has his hero Merek explain that he is ready for the fourteenth century, since he knows "Old English and Middle French."[75]His phonetic transcriptions of Middle English are equally painful,[76] made even worse by an attempt at an Irish dialect.

As a typical postmodern pastiche he includes a mysterious Green Knight, "a huge man nearly 7 feet tall" whose "armor is smeared with green mold,"[77] who carries a "butchering block" and massive ax.[78] But we learn he is really an insane knight who guards a green chapel and seems to refuse to die when his own head is chopped off.[79]

The first third of the novel is weighted by discussions of science. Evil genius Doninger is not advocating time travel but space travel, finding another place in the "multiverse,"[80] using "wormhole connections in the quantum foam," that "remnant of the birth of the universe."[81] Thus what is transported is not the person but "the information equivalent of a person,"[82] and this is done by "quantum computers."[83] A troop of specialists return to the fourteenth century to rescue Professor Johnston. They have thirty-seven hours to achieve this rescue and return. Among the obstacles they encounter is Robert de Kere (aka Deckard), an already aggressive and unbalanced technician who has been damaged by the transport process and who is committed to sabotaging any rescue out of sheer spite. The quest to find Johnston involves mysterious keys, secret passages down stone steps, underground rivers, and a series of last minute rescues – all of the features of the modern gothic novel as readers/viewers of *Jurassic Park* will recognize.

IV.

Perhaps the differing attitudes of these three novels can best be seen if we see how they treat tournaments. Twain finds Malory to be obsolete, not only in language, but also weapons. Sir Sagramor le Desirous overhears Hank's spoken prayer for Gary – "'I hope to gracious he's killed'"[84] – takes exception, and after his unsuccessful quest, returns to challenge him. Given choice of weapons, Hanks uses his lasso and later (when Merlin steals that) his "dragoon revolver."[85] His aim is to break "the back of knight-errantry."[86]

Ford Madox Ford has an equally unlikely tourney in which the two competing ladies, Blanche and Dionissia, compete for the Tamworth-Egerton cross and Sorrell. Indeed, Sorrell introduces the possible idea,[87] and even discovers literary precedent.[88] But the scene is skillfully built. The ladies break three lances and Dionissia wins by unhorsing her opponent. She even overcomes the Knight of Coucy with a skillful swing of her axe.

As we might expect, Crichton is interested in technical equipment. He introduces the training apparatus for jousting, the quintain (also lets us know about medieval archers and tennis). Blundering graduate student Chris Hughes mistakenly picks up a gage and must stand to a challenge. When Marek rescues him and overcomes his opponent, Chris describes this heroic encounter in simplistic postmodern terms "'It's a game of chicken on horses. These people are insane.'"[89]

Hank Morgan destroys the world of knight errantry by first imposing his values on it and then using his modern weapons. He must finally destroy the whole to keep his opponents from discovering his weapons. Though he may criticize Malory, Twain's episodic meanderings make Malory seem well organized. Ford's novel is not only a "Twain wrecker" but in William Gas's description, "a textbook of narrative techniques, a catalogue of resources."[90] Though Crichton may use a few of these narrative techniques, he lays on the quasi-science much too thick and develops characters that are at their very best stereotypical.

Twain uses the past to satirize the present and the past. Crichton seems to champion the past as a means of exposing the limitations of the present, but his understanding of that past is suspect. Each writer relies on the accuracies of his own particular impressions and on his own prose style to present them to his readers. Both Twain and Ford seem to have less faith in historical fiction than Crichton. Twain and Hank both play fast and loose with history. Ford goes so far as to dismiss historical fiction as "a tour de force, a fake more or less genuine in imagination and workmanship."[91] Yet, perhaps because of his imagination and skillful workmanship, he provides us with a sense of the texture and taste of life, not merely a list of causes and issues. In that he may well be acting like one of his favorite painters, Hans Holbein, or at least the Holbein that Ford, the grandson of the pre-Raphaelite painter Ford Madox Brown, understood. "In his monograph on Holbein, Ford sets up a contrast between medieval literature and renaissance painting: "medievalism stands for the love of outdoor nature, whilst the Renaissance reveled in the human form and in natural objects conventionalized."[92] Indeed, this very contrast can be seen in his trilogy *The Fifth Queen* (1906-08). And although he pays some attention to "outdoor nature" in *Ladies Whose Bright Eyes*, which is set in the fourteenth century, his real attention is to "human" experience. Hans Holbein, like Ford himself, "has the saving grace of humor,"[93] something that Crichton lacks and that Twain uses in this novel often without much grace. Ford's Holbein has "the eyes of ... a good-humored skeptic" while the eyes of Durer in his self-portrait are "those of a fanatic."[94] We sense that same kind of unforgiving fanaticism in both Hank Morgan (and perhaps Twain), and certainly in Doninger and Crichton. Despite then his own breezy dismissal of historical fiction as fake or the product of his "impressions," I find Ford the best time-traveler and novelist of this trio.

BUFFALO STATE COLLEGE (SUNY)

NOTES

[1] GBS, "Notes to Caesar and Cleopatra," (Baltimore: Penguin, 1960), 127.

[2] William Gass, "The Neglect of the Fifth Queen," *The Presence of Ford Madox Ford.* Ed. S.J. Stang (Philadelphia: U Penn P, 1981), 215-43; reprinted as "Afterword" in *Fifth Queen* (New York: Ecco, 1986).

[3] Gass, 599.

[4] Mark Twain, *A Connecticut Yankee in King Arthur's Court* in *Historical Romances* (New York: Library of the Americas (Literary Classics of the United States), 1994). This follows the California Twain (1979), but is more readily available.

[5] Twain, 222.

[6] Twain, 224.

[7] Twain, 222.

[8] Twain, 223.

[9] Twain, 223.

[10] Twain, 229.

[11] Twain, 230.

[12] Twain, 232.

[13] Twain, 233; emphasis added.

[14] Twain, 234.

[15] Twain, 294.

[16] Twain, 296.

[17] Twain, 255-6.

[18] From Thomas Malory, *Morte Arthure* VII.29.

[19] Twain, 269.

[20] Twain, 278.

[21] Twain, 83.

[22] Twain, 84.

[23] Twain, 121.

[24] Twain, 125.

[25] Twain, 127.

[26] Twain, 190.

[27] Twain, 433-4.

[28] Twain, 435.

[29] Quoted in Ford Madox Ford, *Ladies Whose Bright Eyes* (Philadelphia: Lippencott, 1935), 3.

[30] Ford *Ladies Whose Bright Eyes*, 14.

[31] Ford, *Ladies Whose Bright Eyes*, 44.

[32] Ford, *Ladies Whose Bright Eyes*, 45.

[33] Ford, *Ladies Whose Bright Eyes*, 21.

[34] Ford, *Ladies Whose Bright Eyes*, 19-20.

[35] Ford, *Ladies Whose Bright Eyes*, 20.

[36] Ford, *Ladies Whose Bright Eyes*, 20.

[37] Ford, *Ladies Whose Bright Eyes*, 7.

[38] Ford, *Ladies Whose Bright Eyes*, 24.

[39] Ford, *Ladies Whose Bright Eyes*, 23.

[40] Ford, *Ladies Whose Bright Eyes*, 267.

[41] Ford, *Ladies Whose Bright Eyes,* 122.

[42] Ford, *Ladies Whose Bright Eyes,* 126.

[43] Ford, *Ladies Whose Bright Eyes,* 161, 167, 171.

[44] Ford, *Ladies Whose Bright Eyes,* 131.

[45] Ford, *Ladies Whose Bright Eyes,* 155.

[46] Ford, *Ladies Whose Bright Eyes,* 247.

[47] Ford, *Ladies Whose Bright Eyes,* 247.

[48] Ford, *Ladies Whose Bright Eyes,* 131.

[49] Ford, *Ladies Whose Bright Eyes,* 331.

[50] Ford, *Ladies Whose Bright Eyes,* 64.

[51] Ford, *Ladies Whose Bright Eyes,* 64.

[52] Ford, *Ladies Whose Bright Eyes,* 98.

[53] Ford, *Ladies Whose Bright Eyes,* 150-1.

[54] Ford, *Ladies Whose Bright Eyes,* 14.

[55] Ford, *Ladies Whose Bright Eyes,* 53.

[56] Ford, *Ladies Whose Bright Eyes,* 53.

[57] Ford, *Ladies Whose Bright Eyes,* 68.

[58] Ford, *Ladies Whose Bright Eyes,* 74.

[59] Ford, *Ladies Whose Bright Eyes,* 82-3.

[60] Ford, *Ladies Whose Bright Eyes,* 91.

[61] Ford, *Ladies Whose Bright Eyes,* 111.

[62] Ford, *Ladies Whose Bright Eyes,* 77.

[63] Ford, *Ladies Whose Bright Eyes,* 190.

[64] Ford, *Ladies Whose Bright Eyes,* 104.

[65] Ford, *Ladies Whose Bright Eyes,* 106.

[66] Ford, *Ladies Whose Bright Eyes,* 251.

[67] Ford, *Ladies Whose Bright Eyes,* 252.

[68] Ford, *Ladies Whose Bright Eyes,* 352.

[69] Ford, *Ladies Whose Bright Eyes,* 354.

[70] Ford, *Ladies Whose Bright Eyes,* 357.

[71] Michael Crichton, *Timeline* (New York: Ballantine, 1999), 55.

[72] Crichton, 479.

[73] Crichton, 393.

[74] Crichton, 233.

[75] Crichton, 132.

[76] Crichton, 215-17.

[77] Crichton, 407.

[78] Crichton, 408.

[79] Crichton, 422-3.

[80] Crichton, 124.

[81] Crichton, 480.

[82] Crichton, 137.

[83] Crichton, 138.

[84] Twain, 74.

[85] Twain, 394.

[86] Twain, 397.

[87] Ford, *Ladies Whose Bright Eyes*, 86.

[88] Ford, *Ladies Whose Bright Eyes*, 317.

[89] Crichton, 265.

[90] Gass, 607.

[91] Ford Madox Ford, *Hans Holbein: A Critical Monograph* (London: Duckworth, 1905), 49.

[92] Ford, *Hans Holbein: A Critical Monograph*, 4.

[93] Ford, *Hans Holbein: A Critical Monograph*, 48.

[94] Ford, *Hans Holbein: A Critical Monograph*, 47.

Mapping the Green Man's Territory in
Lindsay Clarke's *The Chymical Wedding*

Liliana Sikorska

Lindsay Clarke's *The Chymical Wedding* (1989) is a contemporary novel, a post-modern romance rewriting and re-appropriating both contemporary and medieval alchemical metaphors and drawing extensive parallels between a medieval "interpretation" of the world and alchemical arts, and indeed seventeenth-century alchemical studies and nineteenth century Hermetic revival. The text encourages the pursuit into the "Hermetic Mystery," which in turn initiates the quest within the characters' souls. As the lives of the characters progress in two different time frames (even three if one counts the life of the seventeenth-century predecessor of one of the characters), they explore not only alchemical mysteries, but also their own lives. The nineteenth-century story of Louisa Agnew is based on the life of Ann Atwood (1817-1910), the tragic figure of a scholar fascinated with Hermetic philosophy, who agreed to burn her life's work as it was, according to her father, dangerous to the world. In a truly postmodern way, Clarke's novel documents history through stories. The pursuit for the Hermetic mystery, which is carried out by Louisa Agnew and her father, Henry Agnew, also a poet, progresses alongside a mysterious and mystical relationship (friendship, and finally, a love affair) that develops between Louisa Agnew and the new rector Edwin Frere. Full of alchemical imagery bound with literary allusions, Hermetic research is initiated by the twentieth-century characters – Edward Nesbit, a poet who in his time was a well-known figure, and his girlfriend Laura, a potter. They are joined in their pursuit by yet another poet, Alex Darken, who at the time suffers from writer's block as he attempts to come to terms with his divorce. All of them endeavor to retrieve the notes to the lost (burnt) book by Louisa Agnew. Most of their research is done through and within the written culture, hence, the themes of literature, philosophy, and writing reverberate throughout the novel. Alchemy becomes a metaphor for writing. At the same time, the text unwinds, and is finally wound up at the end through the figure of the pre-Christian Green Man and related pagan motifs,[1] as well as the Christian Green Knight. The novel treats history and culture as an alchemical formula, unreadable, incomprehensible, and yet strikingly real.[2] Thus, the Green Man/Knight becomes a catalyst for the characters, uniting the book's Christian themes with the alchemical counterparts. This paper is an exploration of the book's implied medievalist motifs related to the past literary potency and opposed to contemporary literary barrenness.

The Green Man's motif links the pre-textual culture of the past[3] with the textual culture of today. In *The Chymical Wedding*, texts, in some way, correspond to the alchemical elements necessary for transmutation. Hence, a very strong and compelling aspect of the work is associated with literary texts, which comment upon and expand the thematic scope of the book. Blake's *Four Zoas*, for example, draws Darken's attention to his own predicament. Likewise, the poems of Catullus, whose poetic voice echoes in both the nineteenth- and twentieth-century plots, invite parallels between various situations in the novel. "'I found a nice nineteenth-century edition of Catullus,'" says Alex, "'and passed a wry quarter of an hour savouring the acid that the young Roman had thrown at Lesbia in his hurt. I recognized that voice. Failing verses of my own.'"[4] We may only speculate that this is the same edition that Reverend Edwin Frere enjoyed time and time again in the nineteenth-century Munding rectory. One does not have to recall the rules of intertextuality to see the function of various literary works evoked in *The Chymical Wedding*. Ubiquitous allusions to literary works, which are prominent in the conversations of the characters, expand and intensify the meaning of Clarke's novel providing extensive cultural background.[5] They bring out contemporary relevance of the issues they point to; what is more, the self-conscious use of the intertexts places the biography of Ann Atwood in the fictional background. The intertexts, and especially the most prominent one, the Green Man/Knight, feature in more than one cultural context. Just as is the case in other postmodern romances (Iris Murdoch's *The Green Knight*[6] would be a good example), intertextuality can be defined as a dialogue between texts where "the posterior work perhaps has the preferential right of interpretation – but maintains it only precariously."[7] Intertextuality thus has to be understood as enhancing the symbolic level of meaning of the contemporary text, but since it is a two-way process, the older text is also influenced by the contemporary work expanding its own dimension of meaning. Indeed, in a truly postmodern manner, *The Chymical Wedding* comments on the chivalric romance through the situations its nineteenth- and twentieth -century characters are placed in. Its postmodernity is manifested in the reciprocal effect suggesting the reinterpretation of the texts involved. The novel constantly highlights the characters' pervasive love of books. Their love of the written word is likewise manifested in Alex Darken's fascination with Ralph Agnew's library. Having a strong penchant for various Hermetic texts like *The Asclepian Dialogue of Hermes*, Alex, nevertheless, has difficulty comprehending such writings. "'I shifted ground to literature, regretting that the emblem of alchemy were now too arcane to be of service to modern writers,'"[8] he observes, while he later realizes that it is his interest in the Hermetic mystery, his visions, and his dreams that rejuvenate his own writing.

The exploration of the Hermetic mystery, from its onset in the Middle Ages, had considerable appeal to philosophers, as it was supposed to provide the ultimate explanation of the world. Cryptic in essence, alchemical symbols were revealing and mystifying at the same time, as was also the writing of alchemical formulae. The process itself was sacred, as it unravels the mysteries of nature, hence secrecy and symbolic veiling of the truth were always the poetics of alchemical principles. All religious, medical, chemical, and astrological knowledge was enlisted by the alchemists in the service of making this ultimate discovery. The knowledge of such powerful mysteries of nature was not for the general public, hence obscure language and seemingly ill-matched correspondences pervade alchemical treatises. For the medieval church, alchemical rites were pagan, hence the veil of secrecy. Alchemists used pseudonyms while authoring alchemical treatises. Many times, they were persecuted as heretics and practitioners of black magic, and indeed the line separating the art of alchemy from the art of magic is sometimes very thin.[9] The marginality of alchemy alongside the reconstruction of history is a truly postmodern quality of the novel, which provides the (one wants to say alchemical) transformation of literary tradition and, at the same time, grants it parodic continuity.

The reconciliation of the past with the present (Alex has to come to terms with his painful divorce and overcome his writer's block, hence his delight in reading Catullan diatribes against Lesbia) is related to the motif of the Green Knight and the Middle English romance of *Sir Gawain and the Green Knight*, whose story functions as a catalytic converter to the situation in which all the contemporary characters are entangled. The fourteenth-century romance is based on the vegetation myth, hence the importance of the circle of death and rebirth through moral failure. For the twentieth-century protagonists, the Green Man's ordeal is also reminiscent of the revised cycle of the loss (of writing abilities) and the quest (to regain them); the characters' failure to salvage the notes to Louisa's manuscript is then amplified by the conflict between the two men, Edward and Alex. Similarly to the medieval text, reconciliation comes as the outcome of the trial, which the use of the medieval romance anticipates and emphasizes. It is also significant that for the unfortunate and unconscious poets-rivals, Nesbit and Darken, the Middle Ages were the time when poets had an important function in society, as the ones who carried out the process of transformation of the world into the word.

'I'd arranged to meet Bob by the cloisters [of Norwich cathedral] where, visually at least, there was nothing between me and the Middle Ages. Those vaults had been raised in a time when poets were honoured and feared, when they were prized as the living memory-bank of experience. There had been a time too when I was confident of a place among them.'[10]

Pondering on the poets of the past, Alex recognizes their stance by ironically comparing it with his own unimportance. Having an acute sense of his own poetic impotence, at the beginning of his stay in Munding, Alex may have been the victim of the so called "reverse alchemy," the process wherein in alchemical research designates failure, and which instead of perfected shiny "stone" leaves him with leaden hue and with eyes blurred. It is perhaps due to this "reverse alchemy" that Alex Darken is initially stunned and suspicious of Edward's and Laura's endeavors. For him, alchemy borders on the magic and witchcraft ridiculed in literature by such writers as Chaucer ("Canon's Yeoman's Tale") and Jonson (*The Alchemist*). Edward Nesbit patiently explains that the men Chaucer and Jonson met were con-artists, "'lacking the patience to woo the Lady Alchemia they tried to rape her. They failed, of course, and their failure made the enterprise appear contemptible.'"[11] Just like Henry Agnew more than one hundred years earlier, Nesbit rages against materialism, claiming that the only way to save the world from self-destruction is to discover the promise of alchemy, which reunites matter with spirit.

According to one of the most famous alchemists, "many wonderful Arts and Sciences also have seemed to be made appeared to Artists in their dreams; the relation whereof hath been, because they have always had an ardent affection to those Arts."[12] The idea of a clarification of alchemical symbols through direct revelation in dreams and visions was familiar to many eminent alchemists.[13] Paracelsus (1493-1541) developed a concept of *mana*, to the extent that he believed man's imagination holds the power of symbolic causation: "if he [the magus] thinks of fire, he is on fire; if he thinks of war, he will cause war. All depends upon man's imagination to be Sun, i.e., that he imagines wholly that which he wills."[14] The magician or alchemist in this way has control over certain forces which inhere in actual physical objects – he further may control the transfer of souls from one object to another, and to each stage of this metempsychosis are assigned specific alchemical symbols. After splitting with his wife, Alex is scarred and cannot write poetry.

'It was that sense which had brought me to Munding, which had set me hunting the Green Man in the woods. It had been intensified by the mysterious directive of my dream, and by the provocative conversations with Edward ... Only me – my future: Alex Darken taking another step in the daft jig of his life, pushed from the rear by his own dark dreams.'[15]

The Green Man reappears in Alex's dreams with all its mute, pagan and alchemical significance and literary potency mapping his spiritual territory and expanding Alex's perception of nature and life. This interior map of the

Green Man's land then makes its way into Alex's new poetry. In an almost Paracelsan manner, Alex also experiences revelations through his dreams and visions, but in his case they are linked with his yet unwritten poetry. The most potent vision is that of the Green Man. The tradition of the Green Man goes back to the classical and pagan prototypes.[16] The Green Man has been an ambiguous figure since early Christian times when Rabanus Maurus, an influential theologian of the eighth century, claimed that leaves represent the sins of the flesh or lustful and wicked man doomed to eternal damnation.[17] Basford elaborates on the medieval chains of association in particular reference to the Green Man's representation in visual art. For Sadowski, the question of "greenness" is also an important pointer to medieval color symbolism, which was far more ambiguous and elusive than one tends to think, ranging from the never-ending cycle of death and rebirth to the devil dressed in a green hunter's outfit hunting for innocent souls.[18] Drawing from medieval tradition undeniably enriches the book's significance and the meaning of Darken's and Nesbit's spiritual quest. The Green Knight from medieval poems is a vivid figure, carrying an axe and a branch of the holly, both incorporating rather sinister associations. "Holly is a "holy" plant par excellence, as such epitomizing the essence of the Christological experience understood as a voluntary or undeserved self-sacrifice and death followed by resurrection."[19] Alchemical treatises confirm the connection between emerald and gold, exploring divine mysteries in nature, and emerald green is linked to alchemy, as well as to the more general medieval beliefs related to precious stones (cf. Hildegard of Bingen and her treatise on the stones). Green was also the color of the legendary Grail.[20] Conversely, alchemy regarded greenness also as a sign of sickness or decay (not to mention the Christian idea of the rust of sin). However, in many late medieval and early renaissance texts, one finds that greenness is straightaway "changed by our magistry into our most true gold."[21]

> The green image budded in my mind, became the Green Man – that mute, shambling creature, feral and furtive, arrested somewhere along the evolutionary line to man. Green as envy. As you and its callow folly. He was there, watching from my own dark glades. I glimpsed him for a moment clearer than ever before; but then he was gone, slipped away, too canny to declare himself in public. No one's Caliban but mine.[22]

Initially, it is because of his unsettling dreams and visions that Alex decides to join Edward and Laura in their pursuit of the mystery. Proving the strength of clarification as his dreams materialize in waking visions, Alex comes to recognize the primeval Green Man and feels himself surrounded by his magic. He sees the same face in the manuscript in Ralph Agnew's library:

"The Green Man wore a coronet of leaves and a girdle of stems at his waist. The unknown artist had painted the fur with such a delicate brush you felt you might stroke it. The bearded face smiled in its mantle of green hair."[23] Edward, Alex, and Laura share not only an interest in Hermetism, but primarily the same reverence towards pagan symbols. Although Laura is neither a writer nor a poet, she becomes Edward's acolyte and his *soror mystica*, fiercely devoted to the research on the Agnew's papers, and hoping to understand her own past. Laura is, as Louisa was more than a hundred years prior, endowed with psychic abilities, which in itself strengthens Clarke's anti-rational motifs. Each one of them finds him/herself in the labyrinth of symbols without Ariadne's threat. While Edward Nesbit delves into the documents of the Agnew family searching for the traces of Louisa's Hermetic research, Alex is translating her Latin notes. Through the Green Man motifs, Alex Darken, although hesitant regarding Hermetic investigation, recognizes something intangible about the place, something spiritual and haunting:

'I had the engrossed, purposive air of a man looking for something – which, in a way, I was; for among the many pieces into which my life had fallen there was one that seemed to offer some rudimentary promise of renewal. It was that I was after. I called it the Green Man ... And it was not that I expected to encounter him *out there* – in the flesh, so to speak, this clumsy, feral creature sired sometime in the dark between the Fifth Day and the Sixth, and neither man nor beast. But this, if ever, was the season of the Green Man, and this almost medieval wood was Green Man country.'[24]

Linking the alchemical quest for perfection with medieval romance tradition, Edward Nesbit challenges Alex to play the Green Knight's game, the game of resurrection, the testing of mental power and physical prowess, which, in the medieval romance, is ultimately the beheading game. Edward's challenge channels his anger towards Alex and Laura for their sexual transgression. He takes a bunch of holly, and turns himself into a horrifying, barbaric "barely human figure in the long coat, under those green horns, as unnerving as the masked priest at some savage initiatory ordeal."[25] "'Do you remember the poem?' – He asks Alex. – 'The one you couldn't write because a better man had already written it a long time ago. I mean the Gawain poem. Gawayne and the Grene Knyghte.'"[26] Edward ties the potency of the medieval story to Alex's impotence as a poet, pointing at the same time the connection as well as divergence between the medieval and the contemporary images. Oscillating between the real and the imaginary, the medieval romance tackled the issues of chivalry. Accepting death in the beheading game in order to defend the honor of Arthur's court, Gawain proves his super-human qualities. Trying to save his own life in the final duel, however, makes him realize his own human limitations. The beheading game is then the symbol of a challenge received both from the outside world and from the inside.

The place of the ordeal chosen by Edward, the Green Chapel by the sepulcher, is highly symbolic. "The Hermetic sepulcher is the vehicle of the dead Divine Life within us, and at the same time it is the death itself," writes Mary Anne Atwood in her notes.[27] The Green Chapel serves as an alchemical laboratory. It transforms all who enter the Green Knight's game. Such a metamorphosis leads to the perfection of the characters involved, but ultimately it is not the metamorphosis, but the process itself which is important for all the characters. "'Once you begin to admit the truth there is no ending,'"[28] observes Alex at the end of the book. The process of self-perfection and self-understanding is never finished, the metamorphosis is simply there to help in recognizing one's potential. In the Green Chapel, Edward suffers a massive heart attack. Close to death, he receives a vision of Alex asking him to come back. What he later explains to Alex sounds like an alchemical transmutation and perfection of "*natura bruta*" into a more polished human being. For both of them, the events in the Green Chapel signify spiritual transformation:

'[...] Zosimus[29] was right ... One of the texts I didn't show you. Thought it might inflate your ego, but I don't suppose it can do too much harm now. If I can get it right he says 'For the priest, the man of copper, whom you see seated in the spring and gathering his color, do not regard him as a man of copper ...' He hesitated, frowned, remembered,...for he has changed the colour of his nature and become a man of silver. If you wish, after a little time, you will have him as a man of gold.' Then he smiled at me again. 'Mind you there is still a coppery image of green about you; and in the spiritual calendar a little time may be as much as a half a century or more.'[30]

Conclusion

At the beginning, when Edward was initiating Alex to the occult knowledge, Alex picked up the tarot card *la maison dieu* (House of God). In the language of the Middle Ages, the house of God designated an establishment where the sick and poor were cared for, and with one accord commentators on the tarot saw in this figure something rather sinister associated with prison, poverty, and punishment.[31] The tarot image of a falling thunderstruck ruin (also reverberating the Babel story), for Alex Darken was the image of himself "with its Nervalian echoes of the "veuf inconsole" he feels himself to be."[32] For the nineteenth-century characters, the Hermetic quest proved to be a failure; the union of Frere and Louisa ends with a tragic separation and almost ritual self-castration on the part of Frere. Such a courtly love affair once consummated, like the adulterous love of Guinevere for Lancelot, must ultimately alter (and destroy) Camelot, in Clarke's book standing for a certain order of things. Frere is unable to continue his accepted role of a husband, as well as the unacceptable role of a lover; thus, he withdraws and Louisa remains single, but strangely transformed and liberated. For the twentieth century characters, the efficacy of Alex's poetry, in a way, depended on the "union" with Laura. While Alex finds his voice again in a collection of poems called *The Green Man's Dream*, precisely because he is able to enter and win the Green Man's game, mapping with his poems the Green Man's territory, Louisa and Henry Agnew irrevocably apprehend their failure. On many occasions Edward Nesbit declares that most of the great writers were also alchemists (or adepts of the knowledge of alchemy) and gives examples of Joyce, who called himself the last "alchemist;"[33] according to him, the alchemical reading should be applied to *Finnegans Wake* and *Ulysses*.[34] Malcolm Lowry and W.B. Yeats are linked with alchemy as well. In Clarke's novel, thus, unlike in other historiographic metafictions, the literary takes precedence over the historical. The poems of Catullus, the medievalism of the Green Man together with his alchemical symbolism, and connections with other written texts, all take us back to writing and the intertextuality of postmodern romances. Although Clarke's book is an open invitation to the "chymical wedding," it extends the invitation to literature and art which sublimate human life.

ADAM MICKIEWICZ UNIVERSITY

NOTES

[1] The pre-rational motifs in *The Chymical Wedding* are concentrated in the figure of Gypsy May, the statue of the striking Mother Goddess built in the side of the Munding church. Gypsy May brings together the world of visual art represented by Laura and the world of literature, linking the pagan motif of the Green Man with the Christian motif of heaven and all things divine (Piotr Sadowski, *The Knight on His Quest: Symbolic Patters of Transition in Sir Gawain and the Green Knight* (London: Associate UP, 1996), 86-8). For more of the images of lust in medieval churches, see Anthony Weir and James Jerman, *Images of Lust: Sexual Carvings on Medieval Churches* (London: Routledge, 1993).

[2] For more on alchemy and writing see Liliana Sikorska, "Alchemy as Writing – Alchemy and Writing: A Study of Lindsay Clarke's *The Chymical Wedding*," *The Golden Egg: Alchemy in Art and Literature*. Ed. Alexandra Lembert and Elmar Schenkel (Glienicke/Berlin: Galda+Wilch Verlag, 2002).

[3] See the Green Man's images presented by Basford (1998).

[4] Lindsay Clarke, *The Chymical Wedding* (London: Picador, 1989), 121.

[5] During their first conversation, Louisa Agnew disagrees with the reverend's wife, Emilia Frere on the subject of *The Tenant of Wildfell Hall* by Anne Brontë. Truly appalled to find that Emilia Frere looked with righteous indignation at the unfortunate heroine, Helen Huntingdon, Louisa is much more understanding towards the situation presented in Brontë's novel (Lindsay Clarke, *The Chymical Wedding* (London: Picador, 1989), 267). Soon, the readers find out that Emilia has also, although not ostentatiously, left her husband. Deserting him, she had no other reason to do so but her whim to live in the city of Cambridge again.

[6] See Liliana Sikorska's "Constructing the Middle Ages in Contemporary Literature and Culture: The Reading of Iris Murdoch's *The Green Knight*," *Studia Anglica Posnaniensia* 35 (2000): 259-71.

[7] Heidi Hanson, *Romance Revived: Postmodern Romances and the Tradition* (Uppsala, Sweden: Swedish Science P, 1998), 22.

[8] Clarke, 253.

[9] Gillot de Givry, *Witchcraft, Magic and Alchemy*. Trans. J. Courtenay Locek (New York: Dover, 1922 [1931]), 205-40, 347-84.

[10] Clarke, 121.

[11] Clarke, 164.

[12] Paracelsus, *The Archidoxes of Magic* (London: Askin, 1975 [1656]), 46-7.

[13] Cherry Gilchrist, *The Elements of Alchemy* (Shaftsbury, Dorset: Element, 1998), 23-4.

[14] Paracelsus, 47.

[15] Clarke, 214.

[16] Basford, 1998, 9.

[17] Basford, 1998, 12.

[18] Sadowski, 78-108.

[19] Sadowski, 86.

[20] Sadowski, 86-9.

[21] Sadowski, 101.

[22] Clarke, 112.

[23] Clarke, 220.

[24] Clarke, 13.

[25] Clarke, 460.

[26] Clarke, 440.

[27] Mary Anne Atwood, *Hermetic Philosophy and Alchemy: A Suggestive Inquiry into the Hermetic Mystery with a Dissertation on the More Celebrated of the Alchemical Philosophers* (New York: Julian, 1960 [1850]), 594.

[28] Clarke, 539.

[29] Zosimus (or Zosimos), fourth-century AD, was reputed to write mostly visionary alchemical accounts, through which he received the knowledge of alchemical transformations (Gilchrist, 25-7).

[30] Clarke, 516.

[31] de Givry, 288.

[32] David Meaken, *Hermetic Fictions: Alchemy and Irony in the Novel* (Keele: Keele UP, 1995), 145.

[33] Clarke, 253.

[34] Meaken, in his *Hermetic Fictions*, reads Joyce's *Portrait of the Artist* as alchemist drawing on mythical connections between Hermes Trismegistos and Daedalus (Meaken, 122-37). Cherry Gilchrist mentions that Shakespeare and most metaphysical poets were familiar with the arcane knowledge and most of these names are mentioned in Clarke's novel (Gilchrist, 108-112).

Medieval Movie Madness

A. Keith Kelly

Most Americans, and therefore most of the students in university classrooms, have learned the majority of what they know – or think they know – about the Middle Ages from Hollywood. It would be a stretch to assert that more college students have seen *First Knight* (1995) than have read Chrétien's or Malory's version of *Lancelot*, and the William Wallace with whom they are best acquainted is probably Australian. Most instructors and professors who teach in the medieval field likely take in a few films set in or inspired by the Middle Ages, and as a body, we are often quite vocal with our opinions of these movies. Not all of those opinions are positive, and in fact among the greater community of academic medievalists, I would contend that medieval movies generally are not well received. Some dismiss films as Hollywood fluff; others, while enjoying them on the surface, are highly critical of what the movies "get wrong." Even many who appreciate medieval movies make a point of judging them by how much they "get right." In my opinion all three of these views on medieval movies are inadequate because of the basic premise that many critics hold: that medieval movies should be accurate portrayals of history and are judged accordingly.

One need only listen in on conversations or look to on-line discussion lists like Mediev-1 (excerpts of which have now been posted on the Internet Medieval Sourcebook) to get a feel for the prevailing manner in which medievalists treat movies.[1] A film like *The 13th Warrior* (1999) is criticized for its anachronistic arms, *Gladiator* (2000) for its inaccuracy regarding Roman history, and *Braveheart* (1998) for the liberties it takes with what little facts are known regarding William Wallace. One might find praise for particular elements of medieval films – for some of the arms and battle sequences in *The Messenger: The Story of Joan of Arc* (1999) for instance – but such approval is usually couched in a phrase like, "at least Hollywood got *that* right," and the critic will immediately follow up with an assessment of the history of Joan of Arc. I have even read harsh criticisms of the musical scores for medieval films because they are not medieval enough – one review was taken to the extreme of suggesting that medieval films should not have scores at all because the instruments in modern symphonies are not medieval. Comments on costuming, arms and armor, fight choreography, language, and more abound, usually in the negative. Plots are often criticized for being too free with the facts, and characters are disparaged for being too modern, or too one-dimensional, clichéd or overly romantic. And the irony in all this is that those films that present some historical truth, and attempt to depict a believable, if not specific, medieval past, are criticized more harshly than films like *A Knight's Tale*, which can be openly praised (if one were so inclined) because it does not even pretend to be accurate.

This is something that at one time or another we have all been guilty of, I am sure. I scowled when Richard Gere shucked that tinfoil armor in *First Knight*, and I cried foul as loud as any at the modernistic dialogue Kevin Costner rolled out in *Robin Hood: Prince of Thieves* (1991). The problem with this, as I have already mentioned, is the assumption or demand that films be *historically* accurate, and consequently they are judged, good or bad, based upon their accuracy. That is why a film that does not pretend to be accurate enjoys the opportunity to be judged as a movie by itself, because it is not being held to a historical standard. And this, I believe, is where many medievalists go wrong! Accuracy has little to do with the value of film as film, nor does a greater degree of accuracy necessarily make one medieval movie a better teaching tool than another, even in a medieval studies classroom.

The first step in curing ourselves or our colleagues of this malady is to understand that history is not pure science, and in doing so we must understand – some more grudgingly than others – that historians do not have a monopoly on doing or conveying history. Furthermore, not all medieval movies have as their goal historical accuracy and thus should not be criticized when viewers find little. Literature, music, art, all of these have as much claim to being a part of discovering the past as history. In fact, it is only in the modern, or perhaps even postmodern era, that a distinction can be made between literature and history. So why is it that film is not allowed to play its own role in illustrating the past? I am using "past" here as opposed to history with a purpose, and if there were such a word as "pastness" I would here employ it. Having taught interdisciplinary classes I have often been asked by my students for the difference between the study of history and the study of literature. For lack of a better answer I have at times suggested that history is the search for truth while literature is the search for meaning. The sum of the two might be called knowledge. This, of course, is an oversimplification, but it can be useful in thinking about how scholars approach texts and other information left to us by the past. The problem is that historical truth is elusive and at times is as subjective as literary meaning. Thus history can only present a portion of the past, for it ignores the other means by which we may arrive at knowledge. If I were to add film and other art to the mix, a category could be created called appreciation. And so we search for truth, for meaning, and for appreciation of the past by studying history, literature and art.

The other view worth mentioning – though it is by no means a revelation – is that history need not be viewed as static or as necessarily linear. History is a process and a series of connections between different times and viewpoints.

Paul Halsall has termed history a "conversation about the past,"[2] and I find his definition attractive because a conversation has many elements and many participants. Literature can add cultural elements to our understanding not found in reading annals and chronicles. Art offers a visual representation of the past. Film, which, after a century of existence, has certainly claimed its place as a legitimate art form, offers not only visual and aural appreciation of the past, but motion in three dimensions. What no work in print over centuries of writing has been capable of achieving toward an appreciation of medieval warfare, films like *Braveheart* and Branagh's *Henry V* (1989) can accomplish in minutes. That is not to claim without reservation that the representations in these films are precisely accurate, only that film is able to convey information in a very powerful manner that can be more elucidating that the written or spoken word in some instances. Likewise, can one envision writing, sculpture, or art offering a more effective way of presenting the chaos and perilous speed of a chariot race than was accomplished in *Ben Hur* (1959)? In these ways film does have the ability to make unique contributions to the conversation that makes up our understanding of the past. In fact, there are instances when film can achieve levels of appreciation greater than those possible in the written word. Film, as a form of art that seeks to express meaning while at the same time offering entertainment, is in essence not well suited to historical accuracy (aside from the documentary).

So where then does film fit into the conversation about the past, and how can we as instructors best use medieval movies to teach medieval topics? I have already made it clear that a film should not have to be historically accurate, though I certainly have nothing against a film that *is* historically accurate (insofar as historians can agree on such a thing). In fact, a discussion of accuracies and inaccuracies regarding a film can be quite valuable. For all of the criticism heaped upon *Braveheart*, it does present some realistic elements of medieval warfare and tactics, not to mention the spectacle of medieval executions. *Gladiator*, though centered on a romanticized plot that is fictitious, is rich with glimpses of historical Rome. Several of the characters are portrayed quite well as are some of their actions, and while not everyone would agree with the architectural specifics of the cinematic reconstruction of Rome, the resulting grandeur is certainly effective at illustrating how the great city might have appeared compared to the rest of the late classical world. A good deal of the warfare and armaments in *The Messenger* were very good, and a number of military historians, including Kelly DeVries, have commented on such. One of the films that I find most valuable for teaching medieval studies is *The 13th Warrior*, which contains a number of historical accuracies mixed into its otherwise fictional structure. Two scenes, the face washing of the Vikings and the ship burial, are taken precisely from the tenth-century *Risala* of Ibn Fadlan. My students are continually amazed that these two scenes, ones which are almost always picked out by them as likely Hollywoodisms, come directly from manuscript evidence. Historical accuracy, particularly when the movies are considered as a combination of many elements, can be found in many medieval movies, and an appreciation of the accuracies can be very rewarding.

Judging from the reactions most films receive from medievalists, however, I do not think that many of these critics are lauding the accuracy in medieval films, and as I have indicated, an assessment of medieval film that is limited to accuracy is woefully inadequate. Film is much more akin to literature than to history, and medieval films, as participants in the conversation of the past, fit best perhaps into the categories of romance, myth, and epic. Concerned less with specific historical details, medieval films attempt to capture other elements of the medieval past: impressions of a pagan past, Christianity, heroism, cultural developments like nationalism, and of course the political evolution of the Western. An examination of these elements unavoidably transcends any one period in history and thus to confine a film to one historically accurate period limits its efficacy. Many of the supposed inaccuracies in medieval films are in fact successful efforts to render truths of another sort.

Consider for example the anachronistic collection of armor present among the company of Vikings in *The 13th Warrior*. Buliwyf, the Beowulf analog in the film, is clad in a gilded breastplate of the type found in the late Middle Ages, not the Viking Era. While this is certainly not accurate, it does reflect the importance of arms and armor in creating identity in medieval epic and romance. By presenting Buliwyf in such an advanced and visually impressive costume, the filmmakers have identified him with the heroic tradition. Like Achilles, Gawain, and the Red Cross Knight of literary fame, Buliwyf is readily identifiable as a member of the class of heroes who possess arms of great worth and exceptional appearance. Furthermore, a discussion of *The 13th Warrior* and its relationship with *Beowulf*, with Viking and Muslim contact in Western Asia, and the way in which the modern world perceives the Vikings, is constructive and often, I have found, leads students toward a greater appreciation of medieval literature and history. If viewed in connection with some modern images of Vikings, for instance, alongside Andrew Wawn's recent book, *The Vikings and the Victorians*,[3] a fascinating image of the present creating the past will unfold. I have had more than one student, after watching *The 13th Warrior*, turn toward, or even return to *Beowulf*, with genuine enthusiasm. This particular film can also be used as a tool to direct students toward primary source material that is often under appreciated, Arab sources, letting them know that Medieval Europe was not a homogeneous culture but was, in fact, a time when numerous disparate cultures were being defined.

Material and visual considerations, like Buliwyf's armor, are certainly not the only areas in which seeming inaccuracy can work to achieve an accurate portrayal of the medieval period. *Braveheart* may not be a completely accurate portrayal of the William Wallace of the late thirteenth century, but why should it be? The medieval source for the film is not historical but literary: the late fifteenth-century poem about Wallace by Blind Harry. In the poem, we do find much of the nationalism, the heroism, and even some of the romance present in *Braveheart*. While imperfect as a depiction of the time in which the historical Wallace lived, *Braveheart* is an excellent rendering of the ideas and sociology of the late Middle Ages. The fact that Blind Harry used Wallace to represent the ideologies of his own time does not make the film any less historical or, for that matter, less medieval. In turn, modern filmmakers use the tale to comment upon and in some ways reflect the conflict between England and Celtic Britain in the twentieth century, resulting in a villainization of the English by Celtic cultures that has been a pattern for centuries. This flouting of certain historical specifics does not make the film less valuable as a tool for understanding the past but shows the manner in which history is a dynamic continuum.

One of the values of film, like any art form, is that it allows the filmmaker to comment effectively upon one time period, perhaps his or her own, by presenting an alternate setting that might have particular resonance. By clothing modern issues in medieval garb a filmmaker may take advantage of certain tropes and ideals that are associated with the Middle Ages. When teaching I often address these very issues, asking what values are being associated with the Middle Ages, and more importantly, why has the Middle Ages been selected to demonstrate certain themes, be they medieval or modern. Heroism, gender relationships, loyalty, kinship, and religion are all topics that can be discussed in association with medieval films. Even a movie like *First Knight* has merits, for while I find this to be entirely a modern film it retains an Arthurian setting. A discussion of the elements of Arthurian romance and their relationship to modern romance can prove quite fruitful in the classroom. Films such as this reflect the period in which they were made as well as the manner in which modernity views the Middle Ages. In the case of *First Knight*, the filmmakers have sampled from a wide scope of history: a romantic, rather eighteenth-century vision of the Arthurian Middle Ages is used as a backdrop for a modern romance that cheers individualism, celebrates passion over marriage, and even introduces a sort of democracy to Camelot. I have found such an approach to be very well received by my students and often results in a level of engagement with the actual past that surpasses that achieved by simply looking at accurate history. It also allows me to stomach *First Knight*.

This retelling of the present by using the past is worth a closer look by any medievalist, and not only for the reasons I have identified. For example, in addition to a reworking of Blind Harry, *Braveheart* becomes an outstanding example of medieval-style creation, because it in effect mirrors the way in which medieval authors themselves conversed about their own past and present. Blind Harry was not alone among medieval writers in reaching back into history to comment upon current events. This description in fact fits much of medieval artistic creation. Do we dismiss Chaucer's *Knight's Tale*, because while it is supposedly set in ancient Greece, Palamon and Arcite are clearly medieval knights? Do we scoff at the presence of medieval weaponry and tournaments in Theseus's arena? Why do we not criticize *The Song of Roland*? It is certainly not accurate in its history, its arms, its portrayal of Islam, or just about anything. We do not condemn these storytellers because it is an accepted part of the tradition of medieval storytelling that authors use the past to comment upon the present, and in so doing they reveal truths about both. Yet we are reluctant to give our modern day skalds the same artistic license.

Let us step back and consider for a moment the theatrical film for which so many medievalists seem to be clamoring. Let us use the history of William Wallace and rewrite *Braveheart* as a historically accurate film. Of course, the first thing to go must be the title. It is overly romantic and simply a little schmaltzy. Next go the kilts, which of course would not have been worn in thirteenth-century Scotland. The romance? Out. Now the language ... uh oh, I do not know about you gentle people, but I have read Middle Scots and find it to be no simple venture, and that is without the added difficulty of a Scotsman speaking it! Even the Middle English might not go over so well in the theatre, even with the likes of us. Can we imagine Longshanks uttering a phrase like, "Whan that Aprille with his shoures soote, the highlands grene hath perced to the roote, then will I Scottish blood like sweet licours, maken red to run on springes floures." So is it truly historical accuracy that we want? Or is it rather that we are so fascinated by the Middle Ages that we long to have medieval movies live up to our visions of the time – to somehow give value to the knowledge that we spend our lives exploring, appreciating and disseminating among all who will bend an ear to our lectures or cast their eyes over our writings?

The truth as I see it is that for these very reasons we should embrace medieval movies, especially as teachers. The numerous ways in which film can depict aspects of the Middle Ages allow us the opportunity not only to experience a vision of the period that we study, but also to open a dialogue between our students and ourselves. We should welcome the contributions that films make to the mythographic work of understanding the past and applying it to the course of human history, including the present. I would also argue that understanding history as a three-dimensional cultural development, whereby the past is always viewed in relation to the present viewing, it is a more productive way to teach than presenting history as a linear progression of fact. This model allows history to become dynamic in the present and thus permits our students to become active participants. Pierre Sorlin has written that, "history is society's memory of its past, and the functioning of this memory depends on the situation in which society finds itself."[4] In this way the medieval world in film not only mirrors the modern world by standing in apposition to it, but also serves as a revealing point of opposition. Thus a filmmaker can use the recognizable elements and ideals of both worlds to express ideas about human history as a whole.

This last point seems to be readily accepted by even the grumpiest medievalist when it comes to films that do not even pretend to be accurate depictions of a medieval past. Films like *Excalibur* (1981) are seldom criticized for being inaccurate because they unashamedly foreground their status as myth and heroic romance.[5] But they draw as much upon the medieval past as films that are criticized, the only difference being that they draw not upon the history but the other elements used in understanding the past: literature, art and myth. *Excalibur*, *The Fisher King* (1991), even a film like *The Lord of the Rings: The Fellowship of the Ring* (2001), which is only influenced by a medieval background, are films that use the Middle Ages to strike chords with viewers. They dip into the cauldron of myth – to borrow a phrase from Tolkien – and come out with a ladle-full of medievalisms (though not necessarily medieval truths). The Middle Ages has the ability to convey certain ideas better than any other period in our past. While many of these are romanticized, they are not necessarily fictional. The Middle Ages succeeds in being many things for a modern audience: a mythic world where archetypal individuals or even archetypal cultures can take believable form, a realm where spirituality and even magic can be accepted without question, a time of uncomplicated heroism, of visceral violence, of injustice, of moral rigor, and of depraved fanaticism. The Middle Ages can be all of these *in addition to* a period of history to be explored on a critical and scholarly level. But to ignore the former out of a sense of respect for the latter is to ignore an avenue down which we can lead our students toward a genuine appreciation of a very real period of our own history. If a portal to knowledge is open, we should not hesitate to take as many people through as we can. In so doing, we can help them to discern what is and is not accurate, what is being suggested and what insights can be gained from modern views of the Middle Ages.

Without doubt, movies pose an interesting challenge to teachers of medieval studies; the one thing we cannot do is ignore them or dismiss them, because our students do not.

SAINT LOUIS UNIVERSITY

NOTES

[1] Paul Halsall, "Medieval History in the Movies." *Internet Medieval Sourcebook*, Fordham University, (1996, rev. 2002).<http://www.forham.edu/halsall/med.films.html#vikings>.

[2] Paul Halsall, "Myth, Epic and Romance: Medieval History in Film," University of Northern Florida (2002). <http://www.unf.edu/classes/medieval/film>.

[3] Andrew Wawn, *The Vikings and the Victorians* (Cambridge: D.S. Brewer, 2000).

[4] Pierre Sorlin, *The Film in History: Restaging the Past* (Oxford: Basil Blackwell, 1980), 16.

[5] Arthur Lindley, "The Ahistoricism of Medieval Film," Latrobe Unversity, Australia (1998), <www.latrobe.edu.au/screeningthepast/firstrelease/fir598/Alfr3a.htm>.

Dualistic Particulars:
How Mystical and Metaphysical Literatures Demand Differentiation of Erotic Profanities

Hailey Haffey

Medieval Christian literature is rich in odd combinations of holiness, violence, and erotic love. This trend continues into the Renaissance through the piously sexy work of metaphysical poets such as John Donne and Andrew Marvell. These groups are a critical pair in the study of mystical literature because their encounters with the sacred consistently rely on obscene and taboo imagery. In the social climate of these writers, such imagery was classed as profane because it incorporated violence and eroticism, which were considered to be unholy. Thus these constant pairings of sacred and profane are problematic for the modern study of mystical literature where non-dualism is a controversial criterion. Scholars from William James to Robert Forman have sought to define a fundamental mystical experience which is characterized by a collapse of boundaries regarding time, idea, and space. This collapse produces a feeling of oneness in the mystic, an experience of non-dualism. In effect, a scholar seeking to place the core mystical template over the Western experience may deduce that medieval and metaphysical associations of the sacred with the profane may seem to make that which was formerly classified as profane sacred by association. This would dissolve boundaries between sacred and profane and finally seem to produce non-dualistic mystical unity.

If the medieval and metaphysical writers' encounters of the sacred were read in this non-dichotomous way, indeed their mysticism would seem to fit a universal mystical pattern. However, such an interpretation of these Western mystics is a misinterpretation; moreover this misinterpretation is based on a misunderstanding of the ways these Western mystics use *types* of the profane in relation to the sacred. That is, these writers use certain profanities to invoke the sacred, but their use of profanity is always limited. Ultimately, they never employ profanities such sacrilege and utter cruelty. Thus the peril of essentializing the profane is nowhere more apparent than in the contrast between the profanity that attacks the sacred, and the profanity that invokes the sacred.

The notion that some profanities are too grave to be designated as sacred, or even associated with the sacred, may seem obvious. But what seems obvious is grayed when notions of sanctity and profanity are continually paired up metaphorically. This distinction can also be grayed when the boundaries of Eastern non-dualistic mysticism are superimposed on Western traditions. Such conflation appears when scholars of mysticism use deconstructive approaches in an attempt to define an essential mystical experience.[1] Only a serious investigation into the particulars of profanity can prevent dangerous misclassification regarding profanity's relationship to the sacred. For example, mystical erotic poetry from Teresa of Avila to Andrew Marvell is violent and obscene at times, but there is a creative element to their works that always communicates a consecration of the subject. Because of cultural biases toward a prudish version of the holy, we do not realize that the language of the mystics is consistent in admitting only certain parts of the profane into the tent of the sacred, and that instead of indicating paradox, this indicates misclassification certain fleshy, violent, grotesque, and sexual elements of the human experience. A paradoxical union of sacred and profane could only take place if the mystical experience could be described in absolute negative terms. Such a description would be hopeless and antithetical to the Western mystic's essence. For the Western mystics, absolute negatives are reserved for vision perdition, damnation, and wickedness.

Profanities that attack the sacred are abundant in the writings of French writer and pornographer, Marquis de Sade and in fact it is useful to examine Sade's particular brutality when studying profanity and mysticism. Sixteenth-century mystic John of the Cross speaks of God as one who wounds his heart, refusing to make it heal, but the profane in this scenario is completely unrelated to Sade's profanity, which includes descriptions of a man stretching a woman on a cross and breaking her limbs.[2] Because the specific violence and Eros in the poetry of the medieval mystical and metaphysical writers are a far cry, in regard to both form and intent, from the destructive prose of Sade, the necessity for differentiating the profane can be elucidated through a comparative analysis of these two groups of literatures. This analysis effectively establishes parameters around types of profanity because of the similarities and differences in five themes common to both Sade and the Western mystics. The subjects include: 1) the relationship between the physical and the spiritual aspect of humans, 2) the end result of violence in described erotic profanity, 3) the dualistic depictions of union and isolation surrounding the erotic experience, 4) depictions of evil, and 5) biographical accounts of religious or sacrilegious eccentricity between the two sets of writers.

The result of this analysis is that the Western category of the profane can be differentiated into the two respective categories "creative profanity" and "destructive profanity." Creative profanity is constituted by that use of violence and eroticism that leads to connection with the sacred, while destructive profanity ends in destruction or evil itself. Because the Western mystics always exclude utterly destructive profanity from encounters of the sacred, their world remains dualistic and can never be classed in a universal non-dualistic mystical template.

The first category of analysis concerns relationships between soul and body. In her *Meditations on the Song of Songs*, sixteenth-century Spanish mystic Teresa of Avila challenges people who avoid the biblical passage's erotic language. Teresa defends the sensuality of the text and demonstrates that it is important to the mystical account as she cites the *Songs* line, "Let him kiss with the kiss of his mouth. Your breasts are better than wine."[3] She continues by musing whether the bride in the *Song of Songs* was, "asking for that union so great that God became man."[4] Contrary to what scholars such as Evelyn Underhill have attested, that "the articulate mystic ... sometimes forgets to explain that his utterance is but symbolic," Teresa's comments affirm the importance of uniting the physical and the spiritual divine union.[5] By specifying that such a combination of body and soul might invite God into the physical realm of existence, Teresa is recalling the divine Incarnation of Christ and thus asserting that God can physically ravish the human being in its entirety, body and soul. Because of the Immaculate Conception's production of truly human and truly divine progeny would have been critical to Teresa's faith, it is clear that Teresa is not mistakenly describing union with God in physically erotic terms. She is consciously not labeling sexuality in general as unholy or perilous. Rather, Teresa is implying that the use of the flesh in a creative context is sacred. Creation mimics the divine, for in Teresa's tradition, God created life. So to use the flesh in a way that would create either human progeny or spiritual epiphany must be acceptable, even blessed. Thus, for Teresa, physical Eros is always sacred in a particular context; this particular context is the creative context.

Like Teresa of Avila, Renaissance writer Andrew Marvell's poems also use the profane to contribute to experiences of the sacred. For example, Marvell's piece *To His Coy Mistress* is a seduction poem that couples images of a transpiring soul with a body's radiation of desire. But Marvell's poetry also deals with destructive profanities and just so, his poem *A Dialogue Between the Soul and Body* perfectly complements Teresa's mediations on the *Song of Songs*. But instead of lauding the creative type of profanity that enables connection with the divine, in this case, Marvell warns against a destructive profanity that will threaten any experiences of the sacred. He depicts a tortured soul struggling because of its relationship to the body; the soul laments that after being ill, "What's worse [is] the cure; / And, ready oft the port to gain, / Am shipwrecked into health again."[6] Body matches the lament, and hopelessly questions, "What but a soul could have the wit / To build me up for sin so fit?" Thus the critical function of *A Dialogue of the Soul and Body* is that it demands that audiences perceive a dividing line between the ways profanity is

used in the context of the Western Mystical experience because the same
author, who in other cases exalts in the potential of physical and spiritual to
summon the sacred, is here despairing that certain profanities jeopardize the
holy.

Sadistic profanity seems to encompass the sort of "sin" that Marvell's
tormented soul warns against in *A Dialogue Between the Soul and the Body*.
Though Sade refers to the sacred in the midst of his profanities, his use of
violence and eroticism are always intended to thwart any sort of unitive
experience of the divine. Moreover, Sade creates a relationship between the
spiritual and the physical dimensions of man that is dark, and exalts a lust for
utter desecration. In *120 Days of Sodom*, Sade declares, "There is a kind of
pleasure which comes from sacrilege or the profanation of the objects offered
us for worship."[7] In effect, it is apparent that Teresa describes harmony
among God, body and soul through creative profanity, and that
correspondingly, Marvell warns against risking such a harmony through
engaging in destructive profanity. Finally, Sade describes the sacrilege that
always results when destructive profanity is privileged.

The second category for analysis includes the function of violence in
relationship to the profane. Phallic imagery pervades the writing of both the
metaphysical poets and the medieval mystics. In the *Book of Her Life*, Teresa
describes spiritual ecstasies, writing that the Lord would give her visions of a
beautiful angel in bodily form who would stand next to her with a fire-tipped
arrow. Teresa emphasizes both the physicality and the beauty of the angel,
and then she explains, "It seemed to me that this angel plunged the dart
several times into my heart and that it reached deep within me. When he drew
it out, I thought he was carrying off with him the deepest part of me; and he
left me all on fire with great love of God."[8] Teresa goes on to detail how the
pain of this experience was so great that she moaned, and that the pain was so
sweet she would not want it taken away. She also asserts that while the pain is
spiritual, the body felt its depths as well, even to great extents. Teresa's stress
on the physical in this incident is critical. This mystical encounter is a sort of
rape wherein God impregnates Teresa with divine love that she bears through
physical pain. Again, this is a hearkening to the Incarnation and a reiteration
that the Western mystical experience often relies in the joining together of the
physical and the spiritual. But this experience is also a reiteration that, though
such unions involve the flesh, the flesh is used to a fruitful end and is thus
not a threat to the holy. Because the flesh in this context is not a threat to the
holy, the dichotomy of holy versus unholy is maintained, and the experience
must be considered intensely dualistic.

Like Teresa, John Donne uses creative profanity to conjure divine love in
his poem, *The Exstasie*. To begin, the poem's title is an obvious pun on an

erotic experience and a spiritual experience. As is characteristic of Donne, the poem continues to describe a sexual experience in spiritual terms. What is especially interesting for this particular analysis of the sacred and the profane is Donne's metaphor for the phallus. He uses the term "violet" in two places, one in the first quatrain, where he writes, "Where, like a pillow on a bed, / A pregnant bank swel'd up to rest / The *violet's* reclining head, / Sat we two, one anothers best."[9] He uses the term again beginning at line 36 where he writes, "A single *violet* transplant, / The strength, the color, and the size / (All which before was poor and scant) / Redoubles still and multiplies." The Latin root for the term violet is *viola*, which is cognate with the Latin *violatum*, which is related to *vis* or "force." These are connected to the modern term *violence*. Donne's implication here is that the sacred union of lovers is contingent on a certain force – a phallic force. This imagistic assertion confirms what Teresa implicitly expressed in her account of God's arrow penetrating her heart. The key point here is that Donne's phallic force, like the one Teresa describes in God's arrow, is a creative force. Moreover, the face that the root of his euphemism is cognate with the root of today's term violence should not cause the poem to be read with today's destructive connotation. It is the same with arrow in Teresa's story. In both of these accounts, use of violent and erotic creative profanity produces experiences of the sacred.

Sadistic profanity, on the other hand, is quantitatively different in every form from type of profanity described in the ecstasies of Teresa of Avila and John Donne. Fore instance, just as often as images of violence are used in Donne's poem, just as many images are used of pregnancy. The already mentioned "pregnant bank swelled" of Donne's first quatrain can be contrasted with de Sade's imagery, in *120 Days of Sodom*, which narrates fictitious sexual encounter where a girl feigns dead so a man can engage in a role play of pseudo-necrophilia. Before performing intercourse on the mock corpse, the man cries, "Pregnant? No … what a pity," and then at another point continues the fantasy, declaring, "Good God, if only I had killed her, if only I had been the one."[9] The violence in this Sadistic encounter is purely destructive as opposed to Donne's productive violence, which results in the union of souls. Moreover, Sade's irreverent approach to the erotic encounter is also antithetical to the conceptive act of an arrow inseminating Teresa's heart with the love of God. Thus again it is apparent that through the medieval mystics and metaphysical poets use images of the flesh, eroticism, and violence, their descriptions always remain utterly distinct from Sade's.

The third area of differentiating the profane deals with *unity*. In *120 Days of Sodom*, Sade wrote, "Any enjoyment is weakened when shared."[10] Correspondingly, in *Philosophy in the Bedroom*, Sade declared, "What does one want when one is engaged in the sexual act? That everything around you give you its utter attention, think only of you, care only for you ... every man wants to be a tyrant when he fornicates."[11] The self-absorption in de Sade's writing can be contrasted with John of the Cross's poem, *Dark Night of the Soul*. In the fifth stanza, we see how the experience of consummation with the divine is articulated as physical Eros, "O dark of night, my guide! / Night dearer than anything all your dawns discover! / O night drawing side to side / The loved and the lover – She that the lover loves, lost in the lover!"[12] John Donne similarly remarks in *The Ecstasy* that love "interanimates two souls." Both the mysticisms of John of the Cross and John Donne are thus characterized by full communion in a mystical marriage. This communion is diametrically opposed to Sade's isolated hedonism. Even Andrew Marvell's forceful notion of union in *To His Coy Mistress*, uses language indicating two-part participation in the erotic experience; his violence is tempered with affection and ends in "life." For instance, he writes, "Let us roll all our strength and all / Our sweetness up into one ball, / And tear our pleasures with rough strife, / Through the iron gates of *life*." Obviously Sade's erotic profanities conclude in isolation, while mystics aspire to communication. Again, the essences of these respective profanities diverge in terms of both structure and consequence; this divergence amounts to an irreconcilable dualism.

The fourth category of comparison is the location of evil in the literature of the two groups. Unlike Sade, the language of the medieval mystical union with the divine never signifies unity with what the West considers evil, as is apparent in Mechtilde of Magdeburg's contrasting descriptions of mystical union and Hell in her narrative, *The Flowing Light of The Divine Godhead*. In this piece, the thirteenth-century German mystic discusses hell as the city named "eternal hate," and continues with "How hell roars / and moans within itself. / And how the devils brawl / with the souls, and how these boil and roast, and how they swim and wade in the stink and the swamp."[13] Conversely, she portrays the wounded Christ being suckled and writes, "Both his wounds and her breasts were open. The wounds poured forth. The breasts flowed."[14] Even though in this case Mechtilde's account of the sacred is dependent on injury, it is apparent that the sufferings of hell are distinct and separate from the wounds of the sacred. Just so, Mechtilde at other times illustrates the soul as wrapped up with God in a Marvellian "lover's ball," and she writes, "The narrower the bed, the more intense are the embraces ... The more she burns, the more beautifully she glows."[15] Mechtilde uses the erotic here, and hence a sort of profanity, but she does not employ evil to convey the holy. Accordingly, the moans voiced by this union are blessed moans of lovers and never the moans of hell. Mechtilde's warnings over damnation in the segment on hell are thus akin to the metaphysical style where Marvell's *Soul and Body* despaired of sin. Mechtilde's differentiation between constructive and destructive profanities in these pieces are also akin to John Donne's *Holy Sonnet #14* which begins with "Batter my heart, three-personed God," and continues to relate that the speakers connection to God is in peril because he is "betrothed unto" God's enemy. Like Mechtilde, John Donne's accounts of divine union employ violent and injurious imagery, such as that which occurs when God batters his heart. Moreover, Donne also maintains the Western mystical dualism because his descriptions of the sacred do not include that which is "evil" unless they are enumerating ways that divine union might be endangered, such as through betrothal to the enemy. Sade makes the distinction even clearer when in *120 Days of Sodom* he writes that, "Crime is the soul of lust. What would pleasure be if it were not accompanied by crime? It is not the object of debauchery that excites us, rather the idea of evil." [16]Sadistic profanity is always excluded from the Western mystical experience. This is to say that Western mystics' use of profanities is not indicative of a collapsing of boundaries between the sacred and the profane. *Instead*, this exclusion of certain profanities from encounters of the holy indicated a misplacement of boundaries in the dualistic category of the profane.

In addition to literary evidence supporting dichotomous or misclassified profanity, it is key to note that even the biographies of the Metaphysical poets (at least those mentioned in this article) and Sade parallel the epiphanies made in their literary comparison. Though it is always a precarious move to too closely associate author with his creation, in this case the result is too much like the literary comparison to be ignored. Donne's life was characterized by spiritual wrestling. He was a life-long misanthrope. Donne had a rocky relationship with the Catholic Church; he also entered a taboo marital relationship and eventually even ordered the creation of a portrait of himself in a burial shroud, which he used as the focus of daily meditations. And while Marvell's poems served his desire to interrogate life's contradictions, he never resorted to unabashed degradation of the world's inconsistencies.

Thus the real life profanities of Donne and Marvell are clearly honest wrestling in attempt to understand the human condition. Sade, on the other hand, did not wrestle as much as condemn. Biographers suggest that Sade had a rocky childhood during which he was sent to live with his uncle, the lusty Abbe de Sade, and later to a Jesuit school where several floggings apparently inspired an association of sex and particularly destructive (and here religious) violence in the young man. One instance in his adult life explicitly articulates the degree of sacrilege to which de Sade would descend. This encounter is the type that demands a reassessment of the category of the profane (since, obviously this situation transcends the profanity of Donne's eccentric mediation on his own skull). The event occurred between Sade and a young prostitute in October of 1763 and proceeded as such:

> Sade offered a twenty-year-old unemployed fan maker and sometime whore called Jeanne Testard the sum of forty-eight livres – an enormous amount to give to a harlot in those days – to accompany him to one of his rented lodgings in Paris. The marquis, prettily dressed … had driven Mlle Testard by coach to a little house … on Rue Mouffetard, near Place Saint Marceau. Sade led the girl to a second-floor room, locked and bolted the door. He asked her if she had religion; she answered that she believed in God, Jesus and the Virgin Mary and abided by all practices of the Christian religion. The marquis then blurted out a stream of atrocious insults … After telling her that he had proved God did not exist, he masturbated into a chalice, referred to the Lord as a "motherfucker" and to the Holy Virgin as a "bugger," and asserted that he had recently taken two Communion hosts, placed them in a woman's vagina, and entered her, shouting, "If thou art God, avenge thyself!"[17]

The juxtaposition of Donne's more innocent, unconventional behavior with Sade's peculiarities problematizes the essentialization of relationships between sacred and profane, and does so with as much clarity as this article's literary comparisons. In addition, Sade's abuse of Testard demonstrates the fundamental difference in sacred erotics and profane erotics by the location of violence, the ultimate fruit of the union, and the lack of amorous quality to the union. In this example, it is apparent that Sade's pure delight in the agony of another is the type of violence that helps to affirm the notion that types of profanity must be differentiated from one another.

In conclusion, literary combinations of the sacred and the profane may produce an illusion of the boundary collapse that would seem to characterize a fundamental mystical experience. However, pairings of the "profane" and the "sacred" in narratives on mystical union can be misleading if the particulars of violent and erotic profanities are not addressed. With regard to the Western mystics, ideological boundaries between sanctity and *certain* profanities only seem to dissolve when we fail to examine the details of *how* and *why* the mystic is using the profane to articulate the sacred. Because the medieval and metaphysical writers consistently differentiate between destructive and creative profanity, it is clear that their sacred experiences both *rely on* and *result in* radical dualism. Thus the medieval and metaphysical encounters of the sacred can be categorized as mystical only if the definition of a mystical experience can include dualism.

MONTANA STATE UNIVERSITY

NOTES

[1] For a critique of such essentializing views of the mystical experience,
see the contributions to *Mysticism and Philosophical Analysis* (Oxford: Oxford UP, 1978),
and *Mysticism and Religious Traditions* (Oxford: Oxford UP, 1983), both edited by S. T.
Katz.

[2] Marquis de Sade, *120 Days of Sodom and Other Writings*. Trans. Pierre Klossowski
(New York: Grove/Atlantic, 1976).

[3] Teresa of Avila, *The Collected Works of Teresa of Avila*, Vol. 2. Trans. Kieran
Kavanaugh and Otilio Rodriguez (Washington, DC: Institute of Carmelite Studies,
1980).

[4] Teresa of Avila, *The Collected Works of Teresa of Avila*, Vol. 2.

[5] Evelyn Underhill, *Mysticism: The Nature and Development of Spiritual Consciousness*
(Oxford: Oneworld, 1999).

[6] Andrew Marvell, *Andrew Marvell: The Complete Poems*. Ed. George deF. Lord (New
York: Alfred A. Knopf, 1993).

[7] Marquis de Sade, *120 Days of Sodom and Other Writings*.

[8] Teresa of Avila, *The Collected Works of St. Teresa of Avila*, Vol. 1.

[9] John Donne, *John Donne: The Complete English Poems*. Ed. C.A. Patrides (New York:
Alfred A. Knopf, 1991).

[10] Marquis de Sade, *120 Days of Sodom and Other Writings*.

[11] Marquis de Sade, *Justine, Philosophy in the Bedroom and Other Writings*. Trans. Richard
Seaver and Austryn Wainhouse (New York: Grove/Atlantic, 1990).

[12] Robert Graves, *The Poems of Saint John of the Cross* (New York: Grove, 1968), 20.

[13] Frank Tobin, *Mechthilde of Magdeburg: The Flowing Light of the Godhead*. Trans. Frank
Tobin (New York: Paulist, 1998), 127, 130.

[14] Tobin, 51.

[15] Tobin, 50.

[16] Marquis de Sade, *120 Days of Sodom and Other Writings*.

[17] Francis Du Plessix Gray, *At Home With the Marquis de Sade* (New York: Simon and
Schuster, 1998), 63-64.

The Mid(Evil) Nightmare of Yesterday and Tomorrow:
Flagg as the Immortal Monster in Stephen King's
The Eyes of the Dragon and *The Stand*

Alissa Stickler

Stephen King, as one of the most prolific authors of the twentieth century, has created hundreds of stories, locales, and characters that have continued to keep readers enthralled, ever-ready to be dropped into King's often terrifying, always enchanting world. One of King's most memorable and repeated characters is that of Randall Flagg, who appears often in King's fiction as the humanesque incarnation of absolute evil. Two of the most notable literary appearances of Flagg are in King's epic technological fantasy, *The Stand* (1978), and his medieval fairy tale, *The Eyes of the Dragon* (1987).

Both of these books are, as critics and fans alike have commented, departures from King's usual fare of horror. Though both of these novels contain elements of the horrific, their narratives are not terror-driven. As Thomas Reed Whissen writes of *The Stand*, it contains "elements of science fiction, horror, myth, epic, and the apocalyptic."[1] *The Stand* is focused on a plague-decimated modern America, where a single slip in security leaves over ninety-nine percent of the nation dead of a virally-engineered superflu, called "Captain Trips." This new America is a barren landscape, where the remaining survivors drift into two separate camps: the "good" faction, rallied in Boulder, Colorado, around a one hundred and eight year old black woman, a prophetess of sorts named Mother Abigail; and a destructive, "bad" faction in Las Vegas, Nevada, with Flagg as their figurehead. *The Eyes of the Dragon* traces a very different tale, set in the fantastical kingdom of Delain, "populated as it is by fire-breathing dragons, evil wizards and a handsome prince."[2] The story is centered around the family of its aging monarch King Roland, as Stephen King "returns to a familiar theme – the timeless war that pits human good against an ancient insidious evil"[3] the evil in Flagg, echoing the good/evil conflict in *The Stand*. When Roland is poisoned, Flagg, the king's magician and closest advisor, frames Peter (the oldest of the king's two sons and rightful heir to the throne) for the crime, imprisoning Peter for life at the top of the judiciary monolith referred to as "the Needle." With Peter incarcerated, Thomas, the younger son of King Roland, assumes the throne, a weak, lonely, and insecure boy who is easily manipulated by Flagg, whose own sole aim is to destroy the kingdom of Delain.

While these two narratives encompass vastly different genres and literary traditions, they do share several medievalist traits. Both of these novels are set in worlds lacking the technological achievement and advancements of the modern world; both are agrarian societies in which individuals grow or hunt their food in order to survive. Both depict worlds and make-shift societies in violent flux. Both also tell the tale of a time and place where magic and the supernatural influence everyday life, often pitted against rationalism, the two concepts acting largely in defining one another.

This essay will examine the character of Flagg in these two novels as a medievalist interpretation of evil, magic, witchcraft, and the (d)evil figure in the Middle Ages. It will first approach medieval influences that informed ideas of magic and evil in the Middle Ages, and how these perceptions have helped to shape modern literary ideas of these themes. In applying these themes specifically to *The Stand* and *The Eyes of the Dragon*, through close textual reading and informed by both historical fact and current popular reception of the Middle Ages, I will explore the character of Flagg in particular, including the ways in which he both satisfies and challenges traditional literary ideas of evil, and the meaning contemporary academic and popular culture interpretations have invested in the archetypal (d)evil figure. This essay will compare and contrast the character of Flagg between these two novels, exploring how this interpretation informs popular culture's definition and understanding of the Middle Ages. Finally, I will approach the unique balance of connecting popular culture with the medieval, while still investing in its perceived "otherness."

Medieval perceptions of magic, evil, and the (d)evil figure in the Middle Ages were informed by a wide variety of influences, including sorcery, pagan and Christian beliefs and traditions, folklore, and heresy, and were further shaped and molded by the social, economic, and demographic changes of the Middle Ages.[4] These fundamental ideas were not unique or original to the Middle Ages, nor are they now, but just as modern culture does, medieval people brought to these concepts their own understanding, and found within them their own meaning. Concepts of evil, beginning with original sin, are apparent in biblical times, as are issues of magic and witchcraft, and the appearance of evil or demonic figures. These elements have remained a dominant force in civilizations ranging from ancient Egypt to the Middle Ages and the 21st century, and while they have evolved, changing and being changed by the societies which have interpreted them, many of the basic themes and ideas have remained the same.

Throughout their many transformations, ideas of magic and witchcraft have consistently included the theory of communion with another, usually demonic, plane of existence, and a presence which grants power. The (d)evil figure, as Valdine Clemens writes in her examination of the gothic genre, "was not usually the devil himself, but his emissaries in the form of trickster demons, who bore a strong relation to pre-Christian elves and sprites,"[5] once again approaching the supernatural connection between paganism and

Christianity. Common powers of witchcraft have traditionally invested importance in dreams, astronomy, divination, spells, and incantations, as well as preternatural knowledge and unnaturally long life, even to the point of immortality.[6] Superstition and heresy have historically often invested witches and wizards with the power to control the weather, harm or kill both humans and animals, and fly, and medieval witches were often accused of holding secret meetings, conducting human sacrifices, and engaging in sexual depravities.[7]

Medieval perceptions of magic extended from everyday life to influence the political and military spheres of civilization, where common practice of kings, princes, and military leaders often involved consultation with a visionary or seer before making political or tactical decisions.[8] From a medievalist perspective, the most notable occurrence of this phenomenon is likely in the legend of Merlin as advisor and friend to King Arthur and the leaders of his legendary era. This concept of visionaries and magicians as consultants to those in power can be seen to reflect much about overall feeling and manner of thought of the Middle Ages, which, as Valdine Clemens characterizes the period, was "a time when the miraculous and the daemonic were experienced as events in everyday life."[9]

There is also a curious duality present in medieval concepts of magic and witchcraft. While such depictions always center on a struggle between good and evil, there is also a conflict during the time period of Christian and pagan traditions, not only in belief structures and dogmas of the separate institutions, but even in their means of representing themselves and recording their own histories; while the pagan tradition was largely composed of oral passage of information, history began to experience, with the Christian tradition, the passage of information through formal, written, and literary composition.[10] In this way, even in their mediums of communication, paganism and Christianity were diametrically opposed belief systems, and therefore, in pagan and Christian examinations of magic and witchcraft, conclusions and expressions of these traditions vary between the disciplines.

The impact of these perceptions on our current society's ideas about magic, witchcraft, and the (d)evil figure in literature can be most readily seen in the portrayal of these issues in current popular culture, including fantasy, sword and sorcery, and immortal fiction. Each of these genres of fiction express the same sense of dualism between good and evil, and paganism and Christianity, that was expressed in the Middle Ages. The fantasy genre and the sub-genre of sword and sorcery, is the realm in which sorcerers, wizards, and magicians are most at home in our modern, rational culture. Even in fantasy and immortal literature, sorcerers and immortals are often isolated, lone individuals, which may speak to modern society's reading and rejection of the magical, and the dying of a timeless tradition.

The fantasy genre is often defined as the writing of that which is "unreal," which, as Didier Jaén writes, "presupposes a distinction between *real* and *unreal*," which, while commonly accepted, is challenged and rearranged constantly within the tradition of fantasy literature.[11] This perception of real and unreal, truth and fiction, and good and evil, recalls similar tensions of the Middle Ages, most notably the conflict between paganism, mysticism, and Christianity over truth and authority. Jaén also pinpoints the disturbing sense of defamiliarization in the fantasy genre as being in its ability to disrupt "our sense of security with common sense, everyday reality, but in doing so it hints at other possible arrangements based on deeper levels of underlying or all-encompassing unity,"[12] mirroring the same uncertainty of truth and authority, as well as approaching ideas entertained by magic and witchcraft of higher or lower figures of power. Looking specifically at the immortal character in popular mainstream and fantasy fiction, Gwendolyn Morgan defines one key role of immortals in popular fiction as their relationship to humanity.[13] As Morgan points out, the alignment of immortal characters as good or evil is based almost entirely on their interaction with humankind; quite simply, those who work to protect humans are designated as good, while those who maliciously endeavor to harm humans are considered evil.[14] Another intriguing idea of the character of the immortal which Morgan addresses is that of responsibility; as long as humankind is ultimately controlled by the actions of immortals, then individual man cannot be held responsible for his own fate, no matter what the results may be.[15] Just as medieval superstition and witchcraft accusations supported crediting the unexplained to supernatural powers beyond human control, so does popular fiction seek to assign responsibility to a higher or lower authority than humankind.

In both his epic fantasy, *The Stand*, and his gothic fairy tale, *The Eyes of the Dragon*, Stephen King offers a contemporary medievalist interpretation on the themes of evil, magic, and the (d)evil figure through the character of Flagg. Through Flagg, both as the modern leader of a destructive faction of survivors, and as the archaic magician and advisor to King Roland, King both reinforces and challenges many medieval perceptions of issues addressed, achieving a new reading of this archetypal figure.

Social and economic conditions commonly experienced in medieval accounts of witchcraft are present in both novels. In *The Stand*, the technological trappings of modern everyday life are completely eradicated in the aftermath of the superflu. Economic hardship ceases to become a factor with the death of the majority of the population, which leaves paper money fluttering in the streets, and the goods in the store windows free for the taking. Ultimately, in the new world left by the superflu, commerce reverts to the individual trading of goods and services, or the sharing of community goods. Socially, the status of the new world of *The Stand* is considerably more complex, an impromptu sociology experiment with small, isolated groups. The survivors of the flue epidemic separate into two polarly opposed groups in Boulder and Las Vegas; the group in Boulder is going about reconstructing society and attempting to build a better world, while the Las Vegas faction is rallied around Flagg, stockpiling military and nuclear weaponry, and training fighter pilots, seeking strong-arm domination of the world that remains. Flagg's influence, however, is felt in both camps of survivors. In Boulder, the influence of the dark man is felt most by those within the makeshift community who have hate and weakness in their hearts hidden behind the smiles on their faces.

The two most notable examples of this phenomenon in *The Stand* are Harold Lauder and Nadine Cross. Harold, who trekked across the country from Ogunquit, Maine, with Fran Goldsmith, one of the heroines of the book, is a young man haunted by memories of insecurity and the rejection of his family and peers. Always an awkward, overweight, bookish young man, Harold's extra pounds melt away and his social skills improve as he and Fran join another group of travelers headed for Boulder, though coldness and unpleasantness remain beneath his overzealous grin. Nadine is a middle-aged virgin, who has been awaiting and anticipating her purpose in life since adolescence, and who discovers she is destined to be Flagg's bride. After striking out against the Boulder community, coined the "Free Zone," by planting a bomb and killing members of the Free Zone governing committee, Harold and Nadine set out for Las Vegas. Within the Las Vegas community, Flagg wields horrifying power over his followers, commanding them in tasks such as getting the lights back on and collectively arming themselves, and punishing those who do not agree or submit to his ruling with torture, death, and public crucifixion.

Likewise, in *The Eyes of the Dragon*, social and economic conditions are far from ideal. It is worth noting that most of the social and economic hardships, in this case, are imposed by Flagg, rather than simply existing as a reality of everyday life. It is Flagg who convinces Roland, and his successor, Thomas, to impose taxes on the people of Delain, unfair taxes which, due to the cruelty and injustice exacted upon the people through Flagg's history as advisor, the people cannot possibly pay. The people live in fear of Flagg, whose voice directs the headsman's axe at a whim, and it is this fear, combined with the injustices under which they labor, that sends many of Roland's formerly faithful subjects into hiding, where they regroup as exiles and rebels, with the intent to throw Thomas from the throne. Flagg is also able to manipulate and control individuals within the larger collective scheme of the castle and the kingdom. For example, at the birth of Thomas, Flagg convinces the queen's midwife, Anna Crookbrows, to bring on the death of the queen with a small and unnoticed cut during childbirth, in exchange for which Flagg had miraculously cured the poor woman's only son of the debilitating "Shaking Disease," for which the midwife swore the magician a future favor.[16]

Flagg is politically a very powerful character in both narratives, echoing the fabled closeness of Merlin to the ear of Arthur, though the means and uses of Flagg's power vary between the two works. In *The Stand*, Flagg places himself easily and unquestionably as the figurehead of the Las Vegas operation. Flagg is politically and judicially the being whom everyone among his followers must answer and account themselves. Flagg rules the new inhabitants of Las Vegas with an iron hand and an uncompromising mentality, keeping his followers in constant fear of his horrific punishments, which can be meted out upon unsuspecting victims for anything from drug use to treason, or even privately speaking against Flagg. There have been times before the disaster of the superflu, as the narrator imparts to the reader, when Flagg has moved behind the scenes, the whisperer that incited mobs, advising men such as Lee Harvey Oswald and groups such as the Ku Klux Klan, simultaneously nowhere and everywhere in the most violent periods throughout the course of American history.[17] As King writes of Flagg, "he had written speeches for those who did speak, and on several occasions, those speeches had ended in riots, overturned cars, student strike votes, and violent demonstrations."[18] An accustomed speaker from the mouths of others, in the newly decimated and barren world of *The Stand*, Flagg finds the opportunity to rise to power unmasked.

In *The Eyes of the Dragon*, Flagg's political influence is much more overt. Through his closeness to the king's ear, and his position as the most trusted and closest advisor to Roland, Flagg also demonstrates his political influence, following very closely in the tradition of medieval seers and visionaries. Flagg stands in the shadow, and under the protection, of Delain's king. As the narrator says of Flagg, "he never came as a King himself, but always as a whisperer in the shadows, the man who poured poison into the porches of King's ears."[19] Flagg also exhibits a strong power for political orchestration, framing Peter for the murder of his father, King Roland, ensuring both Peter's lifetime imprisonment in the cell at the top of the Needle, and Thomas's dependence upon the magician. Flagg controls Thomas through a manipulative balance of friendship and fear, initiated early in the boy's childhood, and places Thomas as king to serve as a pawn through which Flagg can ultimately destroy the kingdom of Delain, the final goal of all his machinations.

Flagg's powers of sorcery and witchcraft also tend to follow familiar, traditional traits, including the importance and power invested in dreams as a process of divination, which are crucial in both novels, and which played an active role in the medievalist accounts of sorcerers and magicians. An interesting variation on the theme of dreams in both *The Stand* and *The Eyes of the Dragon* is that the power of dreams is not available only to Flagg, or otherwise magically-invested characters, but is also granted to the non-magical human characters in direct opposition to Flagg. In *The Stand*, most survivors of the superflu experience one, or both, of two diametrically opposed dreams: one of Mother Abigail, and the other of Flagg. Those who dream of Mother Abigail dream peacefully of an inviting old woman in a rocking chair, singing hymns and accompanying herself on an old guitar, and those who are drawn most strongly by this dream follow it to the fields of Hemingford Home, Nebraska, and onward to the mountains of Colorado. Mother Abigail, in turn, testifies that she receives guidance from the Lord directly through dreams.[20] The other dream that plagues the survivors is that of the dark man, as Stu Redman, one of the heroes of the narrative, recalls, "something terrible, something worse than plague, fire, or earthquake ... *him*, he thought. The man with no face."[21] This dream leaves the collective dreamers feeling terrified and threatened, though the power of the dreams draws followers to Flagg as well as to Mother Abigail.

Likewise, in *The Eyes of the Dragon*, the traditional importance of dreams is reinforced. It is through dreams that Flagg begins to become aware of the plan to free Peter. It is also through identical dreams that Peter and his friends discover Flagg's dawning realization of the scheme they are plotting, all experiencing matching dreams, which reveal Flagg brooding over his crystal, eyes wide and face eerily illuminated in the crystal revelatory glow as he learns of Peter's escape.[22]

Physically, in both novels, Flagg is fearsome in countenance, a tall, dark, and unnatural man, following the frightening appearance afforded such characters by both fairy tales and the gothic literary tradition, both of which, as established genres, hold themselves to be medievalistically referential. In *The Stand*, though Flagg dresses inconspicuously in worn boots and faded jeans, the narrator intones that "there was a dark hilarity in his face, and perhaps in his heart, too, you would think – and you would be right ... it was a face guaranteed to make barroom arguments over batting averages turn bloody."[23] In *The Eyes of the Dragon*, Flagg takes the traditional guise of a darkly hooded figure with a deathly white face and darkly burning eyes that are rarely revealed, who "smelled like blood and doom; his eyes were death fire,"[24] every bit the character of the medieval (d)evil. There is an indefinable something about Flagg that sets those who see him on edge, some barely checked violence of madness that causes them to shudder and avert their eyes, unable to gaze long upon the man sometimes referred to as simply "the Boogeyman."[25]

Flagg also adheres to many other traditional values of medieval magic and witchcraft, including animalism, levitation, and disappearance, all acts outside the realm of rational thought. In *The Stand*, Flagg is able to control wolves, using them as emissaries to escort an insane pyromaniac known as the Trashcan Man to Las Vegas;[26] he is also able to control weasels, pitting them to attack Mother Abigail as she returns home with a bag of freshly-killed chickens.[27] Flagg is also able to transform himself into a crow, allowing him to travel easily and observe both his enemies and his followers undetected. In *The Eyes of the Dragon*, Flagg is not able to take animal form himself, though animals play large and integral roles in Flagg's plans against Peter and the monarchy of Delain. The first time Flagg considers the murder of Sasha, wife of Roland and Delain's queen, he poisons her brandy with the powerful venom of the deathwatch spider.[28] In his dungeon quarters, Flagg keeps company with an unnatural two-headed parrot, which schemes and argues maniacally between its two heads, mirroring Flagg's frustration and indecision as he meditates on how best to relieve himself of Peter.[29]

There are several other unexplained phenomena exhibited by Flagg in these two novels. In *The Stand*, Flagg is able to levitate, raising himself off the ground, for short periods of time at first, then higher and for longer lengths of time as his power in Las Vegas grows, though his ability to levitate falters, weakening in times of chaos and failure. In *The Eyes of the Dragon*, Flagg is able to make himself dim, becoming nearly invisible to passersby.[30] Another common medieval belief about witchcraft to which Flagg adheres in *The Eyes of the Dragon* is an ability to influence the weather, echoing again the powers commonly invested in medieval sorcerers, magicians, and wizards. In a variation on this theme, Flagg does not consciously exercise his power over the weather, but rather is in an odd communion with the elements themselves. For example, it is on a stereotypically "dark and stormy night" that Flagg stumbles upon his long-sought plan for dispatching Peter and seizing ultimate control of Delain;[31] and when Peter's friends are making their way to The Needle to rescue the wrongly imprisoned young man, they are slowed by the worst storm Delain has seen in centuries.[32]

On many occasions in both novels, Flagg demonstrates preternatural knowledge, also common in medieval depictions of magic. Like medieval magicians, sorcerers, and seers, Flagg experiences knowledge outside the realm of human understanding. In the Las Vegas of *The Stand*, Flagg's followers are reluctant to speak against their leader, even in his absence, for Flagg seems to have unnatural knowledge of those who have allied themselves with him, and as one of Flagg's followers intones cryptically to the

Trashcan Man, "'it's best not to ask questions when the hardcase is involved.'"[33] Those who do dare to question Flagg's authority or go against his rule invariably find themselves facing torture, crucifixion, and horrifying destruction at the hands of the dark man. Flagg's ways of discovering information remain, for the most part, mysterious. Flagg can assume animal form, and speaks of an eye that he can send out into the night as an extension of himself, in order to search and observe. "He sent out the eye," King writes, "he felt it separate from himself with a small and painless tug … now he had joined with the night. He was eye of crow, eye of wolf, eye of weasel, eye of cat."[34] Entering into rational thought, much of Flagg's power is also derived from a near-clinical understanding of human nature, which allows him to easily manipulate his followers by playing upon their fears and weaknesses, controlling them with a sense of indebtedness to himself. For example, in *The Stand*, Flagg rescues his right-hand man, Lloyd Henreid, from a jail cell after all others have died or fled, as Lloyd is contemplating fully resorting to cannibalizing the former occupant of the cell adjacent to his own, and Flagg binds Lloyd to himself with this life-saving act.[35]

Flagg's knowledge in *The Eyes of the Dragon* also challenges the borders of perceived human ability. Again following the medieval tradition, Flagg has near-limitless knowledge of spells and potions, including the formidable "dragon sand" he uses to murder King Roland, a terrible sand from the desert of Grenh, which ignites Roland from the inside out, ultimately burning the king alive. What makes Flagg's elevated knowledge unique from that of his medieval counterparts is that, as in *The Stand*, the majority of his knowledge does not come as the result of divination or second sight, but from an intuitive understanding of human nature which, though complex, is far from a supernatural feat. Flagg is able to control Thomas, the second and often ignored son of King Roland, both as a boy and as a man, as a prince and as a king, not because Flagg has other-worldly insight about the boy, but because of all the people in the castle, Flagg understands and gives a sympathetic ear to the inferiority Thomas feels in his brother Peter's shadow, to Thomas's loneliness, and to the boy's desire for the love and approval of his father. Flagg achieves his influence over Thomas much as he did with Roland, by an understanding of weaknesses and insecurities, and by manipulating these to his own ends, to aid him in achieving his own goals. Most memorably, and the name-sake of this fantastical novel, Flagg shows Thomas a secret passage from which the lonely boy can look down on his father in the king's private chambers, through the eyes of the king's greatest trophy, Niner the dragon. From this hidden vantage point, Thomas sees his father as a withered old man rather than as an all-powerful king, by which Thomas learns to feel contempt rather than the awe and blinding love he has always felt for his father.

Issues of unnaturally long life and immortality are also addressed through the character of Flagg, whose age and origin remain indeterminate and mysterious throughout the courses of both novels, echoing once more the legend of Merlin, whose own birth has been highly contested and mythicized. In *The Stand*, Flagg has been a constant figure at the most tumultuous and terrifying times of recent American history, including Vietnam and the Kennedy assassination, though his birth is an enigma, even to Flagg himself. Recalling his participation as a Ku Klux Klan member, Flagg "sometimes thought that he might have been born in that strife."[36] Traveling back roads and decades, Flagg has been known by many names: Richard Fry, Robert Franq, Ramsey Forrest, and, of course, Randall Flagg, initials unchangingly R.F.[37] Following his apparent demise in the nuclear explosion which destroys Las Vegas, he reawakens on a tropical island, born again, this time as Russell Faraday, to educate the native people of the island, ecstatic with the proposition of unleashing his destruction with a newly unsuspecting band of followers.

In the same tradition within *The Eyes of the Dragon*, Flagg has been in Delain for nearly a century, but appears to have aged no more than ten years.[38] Flagg has also been in Delain many times over the last several hundred years, under different names, though in this novel he does not consistently adhere to the R.F. pattern. Flagg had come to Delain as Bill Hinch, the murderous and blood-thirsty executioner who lived on in the nightmares of children, and as a man named Browson, a singer and close advisor to the king; but he always returns with a single purpose – the destruction of Delain. When Flagg has achieved the chaos he has come to wreak and has began to draw dangerous attention to himself, he disappears once more, as elusive as his age and identity, only to reappear in Delain when order has been reestablished, seeking to destroy once more.

There are also several notable ways in which the character of Flagg in these two novels challenges common medieval depictions of evil and witchcraft, as well as variations that bear examination. One fundamental difference between Flagg and the traditional immortal (d)evil is the absence of a designated alternate plane or existence or a higher power to which Flagg must appeal for his abilities. In *The Stand*, Flagg does not feel himself to be a supreme being, and senses that a change is coming from a power outside of himself, a rebirth directed by a higher power, though he doesn't consciously align himself with any greater presence. When Mother Abigail speaks of Flagg to her followers, she remarks that "'he ain't Satan ... but he and Satan know each other and have kept their councils together of old,'"[39] though Flagg never physically or mentally connects himself with any satanic or demonic figure. Flagg senses and gladly uses the powers bestowed upon him, but doesn't know, or particularly care, where they come from, or even fully understand them. Flagg is able to execute various supernatural tasks, and does possess the traditional traits of preternatural knowledge and unnatural long life, but he is never shown in either *The Stand* or *The Eyes of the Dragon* as needing to communicate with another realm or being in order to make his achievements possible. Rather, in speaking to the modernist perspective from which this medievalist interpretation is made, Flagg's powers are largely derived through rational processes and sciences, including power through the understanding of human nature, and both man-made and natural elements, including military and nuclear weaponry, as well as their possible uses, both for good and evil.

This modernist treatment of the character of Flagg as a humanesque evil also creates in the dark man a duality which works as effectively against him as it does in his favor. Though Flagg does possess supernatural knowledge, he does not, in fact, know everything, and he is far from infallible. In *The Stand*, for example, Flagg begins to be consumed by growing insanity, a sense of his own faltering power and, quite simply, of "things ... getting just a trifle flaky around the edges."[40] Flagg's knowledge begins to reveal less and less to him, and he finds himself trapped within his role as a leader in Las Vegas, suddenly owning an operation as he never has before. As King writes of Flagg, "once, he was quite sure, he would have done a quick fade when things began to get flaky. Not this time. This was his place, his time, and he would take his stand here."[41] Flagg's pride holds him tethered to Las Vegas, and the realm of the material world, fueling his insanity and drawing him toward his own destruction. Flagg's growing insanity pushes him past the edge of reason, causing him to lose his temper, and fatally impairing his judgment. One situation in which Flagg's judgment most dramatically fails is in regard to the Trashcan Man, Flagg's once-faithful servant, whose pyromania destroyed the Las Vegas community's trucks and helicopters, as well as killing several of Flagg's followers. While Flagg makes a mental note to deal with the Trashcan Man swiftly, the detail quickly escapes his unraveling mind. As Flagg stands ready to execute three Free Zone representatives sent to confront the dark man at the order of Mother Abigail, the Trashcan Man returns to Las Vegas in an electric cart hauling an atomic bomb, his retribution to the dark man as the Trashcan Man stands dying in late stages of radiation poisoning. Flagg's globe of free-floating electricity, poised for the murder of the Free Zone men, defies the dark man's control, drawing itself to the bomb and destroying Las Vegas and its inhabitants in a single, sweeping blow.

In *The Eyes of the Dragon*, Flagg is likewise unable to see all. The magician remains ignorant of the wrongfully imprisoned Peter's plan to escape and the plan of the prince's friends to execute a daring rescue until it is almost too late.[42] Another of Flagg's weaknesses that carries over from *The Stand* is the fact that his ego, both confident and overpowering, is unable to accept his own ultimate fallibility. The realization that he has been tricked ignites Flagg's volatile temper, driving him into a murderous rage, forcing him to abandon the cool composure with which he had consistently shielded himself. Flagg runs shrieking through the night in his crazed desire to put an end to Peter, splitting the skull of one of the wardens of The Needle, and taunting Peter as he fearfully makes his way down the side of the prison, at the far end of a rapidly fraying rope.[43]

In both novels, Flagg's death, though seemingly inevitable, remains indeterminate, as the dark man melts instead into disappearance, reasserting Flagg's fluidity and questionable immortality, referring again to the Merlin figure, the tales of whose own end vary from accounts of Merlin permitting "his childish lover to imprison him," to his being "pent in a cave, bower, or tree," his demise ultimately remaining mysterious and unknown.[44] In *The Stand*, Larry Underwood, a leading member of the Free Zone committee sent to Las Vegas to confront Flagg, witnesses the dark man's metamorphosis in the moment before the atomic holocaust. As King writes, Larry

> had an impression of something monstrous standing *in front* of where Flagg had been. Something slumped and hunched and almost without shape – something with enormous yellow eyes slit by dark cat's pupils.
>
> Then it was gone.
>
> Larry saw Flagg's clothes – the jacket, the jeans, the boots – standing upright with nothing in them. For a split second the held the shape of the body that had been inside them. And then they collapsed.[45]

In *The Eyes of the Dragon*, Flagg makes a remarkably similar departure, disappearing entirely from the king's private chambers. Thomas draws his father's bow and arrow, firing the legendary arrow Foehammer at Flagg, where it pierces the magician's left eye. As King writes, "for a moment Flagg's clothes held his shape; for a moment the arrow hung in empty air ... then the clothes crumpled and Foehammer clattered to the cobbles."[46] As Mark Donovan comments, in the case of Flagg, "evil is cyclical, and while it can be vanquished, it never really vanishes."[47] In less than the blink of an eye, Flagg disappears once more into nothingness, the ultimately unconquerable evil, free to stalk the world, and King's fiction, once again.

The fundamental weaknesses within this modern medievalist interpretation of the (d)evil figure suggests the formation, and even, on some levels, the acceptance, of a shadowy gray area between the traditionally definitive black and white. In spite of Flagg's terrifying and supernatural power, through these fundamental faults, Stephen King, as narrator, assures the reader that there are no ultimates, no absolutes. For example, though Flagg has lived for centuries, he has not failed to age, and may possibly grow old, and even someday die; in this way, even the magician's supposed immorality is suspect, called into question, counterpointed by the frightening cycle of the dark man's constant reappearance.

Through the curious duality of medievalism, these modern perceptions of evil, magic, witchcraft, and the (d)evil figure as portrayed through Flagg, bring both the futuristic wasteland of the plague-ridden United States, and the fantastical kingdom of Delain close to the reader's sense of modern popular culture, while simultaneously reinforcing the "otherness" of the Middle Ages. From one perspective, literary and literal evils are very much a part of modern society – concepts of murder, political manipulation, biological warfare, and wrongful imprisonment are all-too familiar in the twenty-first century. At the same time, the obviously fantastical setting, whether it be an abandoned America or the gothic intrigue of a medieval castle, combined with the presence of an agrarian and service culture reminiscent of the Middle Ages, reassert the differences between the modern and the characteristically medieval eras. For example, as Barbara Trietel comments on *The Eyes of the Dragon*, the narrative is "based in a remote fairy tale past, [and] the story is free of the pop jargon ... that King has used in his other novels,"[48] reinforcing the sense of "otherness" through distance from current popular culture. The strange combination of these novels relating themselves and distancing themselves from the Middle Ages achieves a great sense of connection, while supporting enough of a difference that both novels read comfortably as tales of fantastical fiction, stopping well short of preachy allegories or morality stories.

Stephen King's fantastical novels, *The Stand* and *The Eyes of the Dragon*, are unique medievalist readings of magic, evil, witchcraft, and the (d)evil figure in the Middle Ages, succeeding in creating a connection and clear avenue of influence between past, present, and future eras, while simultaneously reasserting the "otherness" of the medieval period. Flagg as the medieval immortal monster of yesterday and tomorrow both challenges and reinforces many medieval perceptions, bringing to medievalism a distinctive position for viewing the Middle Ages – that of the unexplained, the magic, and the monstrous.

UNIVERSITY OF NORTHERN IOWA

NOTES

I am greatly indebted to Dr. Richard Utz, University of Northern Iowa, and Dr. Gwendolyn Morgan, Montana State University for their invaluable encouragement and suggestions, without which this essay would not take its present shape.

[1] Thomas Reed Whissen, "*The Stand.*" *Classic Cult Fiction: A Companion to Popular Cult Literature* (New York: Greenwood, 1992), 226.

[2] Mark Donovan, "*The Eyes of the Dragon,*" *People Weekly* (13 Apr. 1987): 22.

[3] Jackie Cassada, "King, Stephen. *The Eyes of the Dragon,*" *Library Journal* (Dec 1986): 141.

[4] Jeffrey Burton Russell, "Witchcraft, European." *Dictionary of the Middle Ages* v12. Joseph R. Strayer, ed. (New York: Charles Scribner's Sons, 1989), 660-1.

[5] Valdine Clemens, "Precedents for "Gothic" Fear: Medieval Life, Jacobean Drama, and Eighteenth-Century Attitudes," *The Return of the Repressed: Gothic Horror From 'The Castle of Otranto' to 'Alien.*" (Albany: SUNY Press, 1999), 17.

[6] Valerie I.J. Flint, *The Rise of Magic in Early Medieval Europe* (Princeton: Princeton UP, 1991), 87.

[7] Russell, 660.

[8] Clemens, 16.

[9] Clemens, 15.

[10] Anne Savage, "Pagans and Christians, Anglo-Saxons and Anglo-Saxonists: The Changes Face of Our Mythical Landscape," *Reinventing the Middle Ages and the Renaissance: Constructions of the Medieval and Early Modern Periods* (Arizona Studies in the Middle Ages and the Renaissance), William F. Gentrup, ed. (Turnhout: Brepols, 1998), 37.

[11] Didier T. Jaén, "Mysticism, Esoterism, and Fantastic Literature," *The Scope of the Fantastic – Theory, Technique, Major Authors: Selected Essays from the First International Conference on the Fantastic in Literature and Film.* Robert A. Collins and Howard D. Pearce, eds. (Westport: Greenwood, 1985), 105.

[12] Jaén, 111.

[13] Gwendolyn Morgan, "Gnosticism, The Middle Ages, and the Search for Responsibility: Immortals in Popular Fiction," *Medievalism in the Modern World: Essays in Honor of Leslie J. Workman.* Tom Shippey and Richard J. Utz, eds. (Turnhout: Brepols, 1998), 320.

[14] Morgan, 320.

[15] Morgan, 320.

[16] King, *The Eyes of the Dragon* (New York: Signet/Penguin Putnam, 1988), 37.

[17] King, *The Stand: The Complete and Uncut Edition* (New York: Gramercy, 2001), 183.

[18] King, *The Stand: The Complete and Uncut Edition*, 183-4.

[19] King, *The Eyes of the Dragon*, 62.

[20] King, *The Stand*, 513.

[21] King, *The Stand*, 111; emphasis original.

[22] King, *The Eyes of the Dragon*, 291.

[23] King, *The Stand*, 181.

[24] King, *The Stand*, 351.

[25] King, *The Stand*, 184.

[26] King, *The Stand*, 615-6.

[27] King, *The Stand*, 503-4.

[28] King, *The Eyes of the Dragon*, 31.

[29] King, *The Eyes of the Dragon*, 69.

[30] King, *The Eyes of the Dragon*, 77.

[31] King, *The Eyes of the Dragon*, 68.

[32] King, *The Eyes of the Dragon*, 329-30.

[33] King, *The Stand*, 620.

[34] King, *The Stand*, 1034.

[35] King, *The Stand*, 367.

[36] King, *The Stand*, 183.

[37] King, *The Stand*, 182-3.

[38] King, *The Eyes of the Dragon*, 60.

[39] King, *The Stand*, 515.

[40] King, *The Stand*, 981.

[41] King, *The Stand*, 982.

[42] King, *The Eyes of the Dragon*, 335-6.

[43] King, *The Eyes of the Dragon*, 347.

[44] Peter Goodrich, "Modern Merlins: An Aerial Study (Bibliographic Essay)," *The Figure of Merlin in the Nineteenth and Twentieth Centuries* (Studies in Comparative Literature, vol. 2), Jeannie Watson and Maureen Fries, eds. (Lewiston: Edwin Mellen, 1989), 183.

[45] King, *The Stand*, 1085; emphasis original.

[46] King, *The Eyes of the Dragon*, 375.

[47] Donovan, 22.

[48] Barbara Trietel, "*The Eyes of the Dragon*," *New York Times Book Review* (22 Feb 1987): 12.

Alphabetical List of Papers:
Presented at the 17th International Conference on Medievalism (University of Northern Iowa, October 17–18, 2002)

Adams, Jeremy duQuesnay, Southern Methodist University, "The Neo-Medieval of the Luxembourg Between the Wars."

Ahrendt, Rebekah, "From Goth to Gothic: New Perspectives on the Medieval Music Debate."

Arnell, Carla A., Lake Forest College, "From the Middle Ages to the Internet Age: The Medieval Courtly Love Tradition in Jeanette Winterson's *The Powerbook.*"

Bailey, Lori, University of Arkansas, "Breechless Cannibals: Chivalry and Rape in Lillian Smith's *Killers of the Dream* and Sir Thomas Malory's *Le Morte D'Arthur.*"

Blake, William, University of Toronto, "The Idolum is the Image in the Mirror: The Criterion of the Postmodern Medieval Concept."

Canitz, Christa, University of New Brunswick, "Filmmakers Contra the Academic Establishment: Claims of Authenticity in Medievalist Films."

Chabrier, Christina Ferree, Duke University, "Postmodern Poucet and Tristan's Transformations: Medieval Sources in Two Short Stories by Michel Tournier."

Cooley, Jennifer, University of Northern Iowa, "Who's Playing? Games and Society in Medieval Spain."

Crowley, Michael J., University of Georgia, "Authenticity and the Medieval in Don DeLillo's *White Noise.*"

Curta, Florin, University of Florida, "Pavel Chinezul, Negru Voda and 'Imagined Communites': Medievalism in Romanian Rock Music."

Flieger, Verlyn, University of Maryland, College Park, "A Distant Mirror: Tolkien and Jackson in the Looking-Glass." (plenary lecture)

Ford, Renae, University of Northern Iowa, "Arthur Up For Grabs: Exploring Intertextuality and Elements of Arthurian Legend in *First Knight.*"

Fugelso, Karl, Towson University, "Robert Rauschenberg's *Commedia* Illuminations."

Ganim, John, University of California at Riverside, "The Afterlife of the Gothic Cathedral: Modernism, Postmodernism, and Medievalism in Contemporary Architecture." (plenary lecture)

Gronen, Billi Jo, University of Northern Iowa and Hamilton College, "Intention vs. Reception: Battles in Medieval Fiction."

Haffey, Hailey, Montana State University, "Dualistic Particulars: How Medieval and Renaissance Mystical Writings Demand Differentiation of Erotic Profanities."

Johnson, Hannah, Princeton University, "The Saint in the Photograph: Sister Marie, the History That Saves, and Another New Middle Ages."

Keller, James R., Mississippi University for Women, "The Power of Horror: Abjection, Macbeth, and Medieval Cosmology."

Kelly, Keith, Saint Louis University, "Medieval Movie Madness: Using Medieval Films in the Classroom."

Klingfus, Michelle, University of Northern Iowa, "Finding Fidelma: Unraveling the Mystery of Tremayne's Medievalism."

Kowalcze, Anna, University of Northern Iowa and Jagiellonian University, "Disregarding the Text: Postmodern Medievalisms and the Readings of John Gardner's *Grendel*."

Krueger, Robert, University of Northern Iowa, "Portuguese Renaissance Medievalism: Sá de Miranda's Response to Empire."

Lampe, David, Buffalo State University, "'The Accuracies of My Impressions': Ford Madox Ford's Re-Imagined Chivalry."

Larsen, Andrew E., "Historical Inaccuracy and Sexual Politics in Mel Gibson's *Braveheart*."

Larson, Angela, University of Northern Iowa, "The Truth About Tomboys: Current Perceptions of the Medieval via the Film *The Princess Bride*."

Levy-Navarro, Elena, University of Wisconsin at Whitewater, "The Disorderly and Effeminizing Middle Ages in Andrew Marvell's 'Upon Appleton House.'"

McDonald, Heather, University of Northern Iowa, "Medieval Media: Actors as Anchors in Barry Unsworth's *Morality Play*."

McKeon, Mike, Ohio University, "The Postmodern Subject in Early Christian/Medieval Catacomb Paintings."

Mittler, Sylvia, University of Toronto at Scarborough, "The Crusades and Frankish Medieval Greece as Carnival: The Postmodern Historiography of Modern Greek Humorist Nikos Tsiforos."

Morgan, Gwendolyn, Montana State University, "Medieval 'Auctorite' and Medieval Books in Contemporary Booklovers' Mysteries."

Morowitz, Laura, Wagner College, and Elizabeth Emery, Montclair State University, "Consumer Medievalism: Fin-de-siècle Paris and the Marketing of the Middle Ages."

Munson, Marcella, Florida Atlantic University, "Writing Against France in the *Avision*-Christine: Politics of Subjectivity in Late Medieval Culture."

Mvuyekure, Pierre-Damien, University of Northern Iowa, "Chaucer in Post-Colonial Africa: 'Creative-Kick/ing Tongue' on the *Canterbury Tales* in Karen King-Aribisala's *Kicking Tongues*."

Neufeld, Christine, University of British Columbia, "The Once and Future Idiom: Monty Python's Paradoxical Medievalism."

Obermeier, Anita, University of New Mexico, "Postmodernism and the Press in Naomi Mitchison's *To the Chapel Perilous*."

Ostrem, Eyolf and Nils Holger Petersen, University of Copenhagen, "Bob Dylan Musical Practices, Medieval Rituals, and Modernity."

Paden, William, Northwestern University, "I Learned It At the Movies: Teaching Medieval Film." (plenary lecture)

Rochette-Crawley, Susan, University of Northern Iowa, "Wholly Ghosts: Genre, Postmodern Transubstantiations, and Flannery O'Connor's 'The Enduring Chill.'"

Shepherd, Mary, University of Northern Iowa, "Knight-Errant of the American West: Medieval Parallels of Chivalry in Owen Wister's *The Virginian*."

Shippey, Tom, Saint Louis University, "Umberto Eco's *Baudolino*: The Medievalist Bestseller."

Sikorska, Liliana, Adam Mickiewicz University, "Mapping the Green Knight Territory in Lindsey Clarke's *Chymical Wedding*."

Stallman, Crystal, Hawkeye Community College, "Arthur Subverted: The Anonymous *Tom a Lincoln*."

Stickler, Alissa, University of Northern Iowa, "The Mid(Evil) Nightmare: Flagg as the Immortal Monster in Stephen King's *The Eyes of the Dragon*."

Straubhaar, Sandra Baliff, University of Texas at Austin, "A Birth Certificate for Sweden, Packaged for Postmoderns: Jan Guillou's *Templar Trilogy*."

Verduin, Kathleen, Hope College, "Writers Reading Dante: Wharton, Wilde, Sayers."

Wheeler, Bonnie, Southern Methodist University, "Postmodernism Meets King Arthur." (plenary lecture)

Wong, Jennifer, Washington University, "Medievalism and the Modern City: David Fincher's *Se7en*."